"This transformative workbook illuminates the path from body hatred to insights, it addresses the complexity of this inner struggle, offering a journe empowering oneself. A beacon of light at the end of the tunnel, it invites the reader to contemplate a more holistic view of *self*, including teachings on the importance of honoring embodiment and our soul. I recommend this book to those seeking wise counsel on their path of healing and transformation."

—**Rochelle Schieck**, founder of Qoya Inspired Movement, and author of *Qoya*

"During nearly a decade of following Kathryn's body image and self-love work, I have witnessed the infinite depth of her compassion for women who wrestle with and feel overcome by unrealistic, unhealthy expectations about the precious temples they inhabit. This book is a gem—an opportunity to experience the work Kathryn teaches so sacredly: finally, truly, learning to listen to and be in a deep, loving relationship with your body."

—**Debbie DeMarco Bennett, BSc**, MA in progress, and co-teacher of dialectical behavior therapy (DBT) skills classes with Kathryn Holt at www.emotionallysensitive.com

"Kathryn Holt's *Overcoming Body Hatred Workbook* is a transformative guide that navigates the tumultuous journey of body acceptance. Its insightful reflections and practical tools empower readers to foster a peaceful relationship with their bodies, anchoring in self-respect and inner healing rather than external change. An essential read for anyone yearning to reclaim their wholeness and live beyond societal pressures."

—**Stacey Shelby, PhD**, professor of depth psychology at Pacifica Graduate Institute, registered clinical counselor, and author of *Tracking the Wild Woman Archetype*

"*Overcoming Body Hatred Workbook* offers us a path back to ourselves. Holt's wise guidance and thoughtful, profound exercises beckon us toward experiencing the body as a source of rooted wisdom—a home from which we can engage life in all its dimensions. These soulful practices powerfully offset the distracting influences of a culture that often pulls us away from who we truly are, inviting deep, enduring, and healing transformation."

—**Linda Quennec, PhD**, psychotherapist; and author of *Fishing for Birds* and *Depth Psychology, Cult Survivors, and the Role of the Daimon*

"Kathryn Holt offers an impressive variety of tools across multiple healing modalities for overcoming body hatred and shame. She also explores numerous sources for our disconnection with our bodies, including our family of origin and our culture. But it's her assertion that our 'true hunger' is to deepen into our souls that makes this book stand out. It's a revolutionary idea, that listening to our bodies is listening for our souls."

—**Jennifer Leigh Selig, PhD**, depth psychologist, teacher, and author of *Deep Memoir*

"With skill and tender understanding, Kathryn Holt blends theory and practice to guide women into their sacred depths to reclaim a sense of being with their bodies and their true hunger from the inside out. Embodied women who know how to journey underneath symptoms of disconnection and internalized oppression are what these times require. This book is a treasure, a companion, and a pivotal resource toward that possibility."

—**Leah D'Abate, MA, LPC, BC-DMT, ACSz**, licensed professional counselor, board-certified dance/movement therapist, somatic psychotherapist, and approved clinical supervisor in private practice

"Incisive, wise, practical, and kind. The weave of myth, analyses, and deep personal inquiry feels like a compassionate friend walking you along a path of healing that you long for, but may not be able to access on your own. Kathryn Holt invites us into a fraught and charged topic with gentleness and fierce assurance: *your body hatred is not your fault*, and there is a way through."

—**Chela Davison**, Integral Master Coach, and creator and teacher of LEAD programs

OVERCOMING BODY HATRED WORKBOOK

A Woman's Guide to
Healing Negative Body Image &
Nurturing Self-Worth
Using CBT & Depth Psychology

Kathryn C. Holt, PhD, LCSW

New Harbinger Publications, Inc.

Publisher's Note

This publication is designed to provide accurate and authoritative information in regard to the subject matter covered. It is sold with the understanding that the publisher is not engaged in rendering psychological, financial, legal, or other professional services. If expert assistance or counseling is needed, the services of a competent professional should be sought.

NEW HARBINGER PUBLICATIONS is a registered trademark of New Harbinger Publications, Inc.

New Harbinger Publications is an employee-owned company.

Cover design by Sara Christian
Acquired by Jess O'Brien
Edited by Jody Bower

Printed in the United States of America

26   25   24

10   9   8   7   6   5   4   3   2   1   First Printing

I dedicate this book to my husband, Fabio, my ever-present cheerleader and supporter. Your own dance with Soul, patience with my process, and belief in me and my writing is why this book exists. I'm so grateful for you and our life together.

Contents

Foreword

Freedom from body image distress comes from changing the way we see, not the way we look.

The path towards freedom takes us into the depths of our very being. It is a path that calls on us to cultivate our inner sight, our insight, as we tune into the wisdom that lies deep within our bodies.

Walking this path takes us on a twisting, labyrinthian journey, where we at times encounter hairpin turns that can shift our gaze, allowing us look at the world we live in from the inside out, rather than imagining how we appear to the world, from the outside in.

Along the way, we discover the language of the body, which is sensation. And recognize that it speaks to us in whispers if we listen, and shouts if we do not. Through the subtlest of sensations, it can tell us when to move and when to rest, when to eat and when to stop eating, when to sleep and when to wake up.

When we learn to listen to our bodies, it helps us listen to the rest of our being. We recognize thoughts proclaiming we are not thin enough…not fit enough…not good enough…as dark clouds that pass by, simply a part of our mental landscape that is ever changing. They no longer have the strength to pull us outside ourselves, convincing us that we ought to be in a different body and be someone we are not in order to belong, in order to be happy, in order to be at peace.

We notice how our emotions are designed to ripple through our bodies in waves of sensation as part of a powerful inner guidance system, steering us towards that which is right for us and away from that which is not. As we see them as waves of energy in motion, e-motion, they cease to become dangerous "things" that can topple our equilibrium. Rather than trying to stuff or restrict them, we can allow them to flow through us without taking up residence in our bodies. They are not who we are.

We discern the difference between belonging, which we have always longed for, and fitting in, which we have been taught to do. Fitting in is when we try to look like, act like, think like, and feel like how we imagine others want us to look and act and think and feel. It disconnects us from our authentic self and our bodies and creates a tension deep within our being.

Belonging comes when we connect with others while remaining connected to our essential self. It allows a sense of peace and comfort to permeate our entire being. By establishing a strong connection with our authentic self, we can discover the body that is our home, waiting patiently to be seen with our inner eyes.

Kathryn Holt sheds light on this journey towards embracing your true self, paving the way for a harmonious connection with your body so you can feel at home in those quiet alone moments as well as in social interactions with loved ones and unfamiliar faces. Through discovering your authentic self and the wisdom of your own body, you can navigate your path back to a sense of belonging—and find freedom from body image distress.

—Anita Johnston, PhD
Author, *Eating in the Light of the Moon*

CHAPTER 1

Body Hatred and Wholeness

When we pick up a book like this, it's not usually for a light reading experience. It's because we are in deep distress and looking for help. This workbook is designed to offer practical help for relief from body hatred, which can wreak havoc on our inner and outer lives.

When I was in the thick of body hatred, I could not fathom feeling at peace with my body. Before I was in recovery from body hatred and food stress, I had a recurring fantasy:

I am sitting in an armchair by a window. I have a cup of tea. I am okay…

That's it. That was the fantasy. My fantasy was that I could sit still, in a quiet moment, and be okay in my own skin without wanting to jump out of it. What I didn't realize at the time was that the ability to sit still and be okay would only be achieved after I allowed myself to be deeply not okay, feel my emotions deeply, grieve what deserved to be grieved, and long for what I long for, instead of simply hating my body. My body hatred masked the depth of feelings that I now experience as a sacred tether to the world around me and to life itself.

When I work with clients struggling with body hatred, I hear differing refrains of this fantasy, but the underlying desire is similar. We want to feel at ease in ourselves in quiet, alone moments. "Confident," "sexy," "embodied," and like feelings might come eventually—but the first longing is to feel at ease, not in struggle or in an endless parade of worry about our bodies.

This ease is not the same thing as unaffected. It is not the same thing as detached. I think of the longing to feel okay when we are okay as the call towards wholeness, the calling from our souls to come more deeply into ourselves and reside in our bodies. It is a sacred calling to live in our bodies peacefully so we can live in the world more effectively.

People who have not suffered from body hatred may not understand how important it is to feel at ease in their skin. But most people I know are quite familiar with constant anxiety about their bodies. If I could offer a magic pill to create instant body peace, most would gladly take it. Unfortunately, no such pill exists. But the insights and reflections in this workbook will give you an entryway to a different relationship with your body. They will offer explanations for your suffering and actionable tools for you to begin paving a new path within yourself that does not require changing your body physically in any way.

Did I lose you at that last part? *Not* changing your body? This is the hardest piece, I find, when helping people suffering from body hatred: it is not through changing the body that our feelings about our bodies change—at least, not in the long term. (Note: I am not referring to body changes related to gender identity, which is its own nuanced journey.) This idea is a hard sell for people who want to heal their relationships with their bodies through weight loss or toning or a new food plan, rather than the work of relating to our bodies respectfully, which is an inside job—the result of working with our emotions, unmet needs, and deep longings.

I am not surprised when clients who come to me wanting to heal their relationships with their bodies expect support for their weight loss efforts. Most people in their lives (and social media) will encourage them to try to lose weight, or get "fit," or make other body-change efforts. It's an ever-present cultural value to be in control of one's body. When I work with these clients, we consider how previous attempts at body change have worked for them in the long run. Usually it's a grim picture, filled with shame that they can't just stay on the exercise plan or the cleanse, frustration that their attempts are short-lived at best, and a fair amount of hopelessness that they might be stuck with the bodies they have.

Then we consider the possibility that they might create a new relationship with their bodies just as they are now. We consider that perhaps their feelings about their bodies might distract from deeper longings and needs (their own and the world's), and that turning their attention to those longings can be life-giving. Our work together occurs in an unusual space of body neutrality, even body ambivalence, where sustained weight loss or fitness is not considered the elusive holy grail of relief.

In this space, our bodies are reckoned with, but not forced into change. Our bodies are allowed to be what they are—the sacred vehicles that we are given upon birth and that we will all surrender at the end of our days. The process is uncomfortable and often unsettling, as with all real change, yet leads to a new way of living in our bodies with respect and attunement rather than control and force.

This is not to say that our bodies don't or won't change as we transform body hatred. In fact, the one thing we can assume in the course of our lives is that our bodies will change. They will age; they will get bigger or smaller; they will die. Our bodies change in each phase of life, even the phase of the month. What this book offers is tools to ride the wave of change, whatever it happens to bring, rather than forcing our bodies to conform to body ideals we have internalized (usually standards imposed on us from outside) so that we can feel more whole.

Healing from body hatred through listening to our bodies and cultivating a relationship of acceptance toward them does not mean that we don't take care of our bodies. In fact, it's the opposite. Because of the cultural pressure to control our bodies, when we talk about listening to our bodies instead, many people imagine that means being out of control, hedonistic, or languishing on the couch. But listening to our bodies for cues around hunger, fullness, satisfaction, need for movement, rest, and touch is really about exploring how to take cues from our bodies in order to be good stewards of our bodies and ourselves.

Where We Begin

The journey to recover from body hatred is as personal and varied as there are bodies on the planet. Yet there are common themes and markers for the journey, and we can ground ourselves in the journey by beginning to understand which themes have influenced our lives and how.

Do you relate to any of these starting points?

- Thinking your body is wrong

- Feeling the need to control your body so it looks a certain way

- Feeling somatically disconnected from your body— not knowing what your body feels

- Feeling stressed about your body

- Feeling—maybe a bit paradoxically—protected from eating disorders through privilege or healthy rebellion against certain body pressures or dictates

Here follows a more in-depth explanation of each of these points.

Thinking Your Body is Wrong

When you start the journey of recovery from body hatred, usually there is a feeling that your body is wrong in some way; perhaps a specific body part or your size, weight, or shape. The feeling and belief that your body is wrong and in need of alteration is often motivated by the instinct to conform socially, in order to belong and to feel accepted by others. The instinctual need to belong, to feel safe and accepted in society, is distorted into anxiety about the body being wrong, with a corresponding belief that if the body could be made to conform to social ideals, you would be accepted.

Consider Alina's experience, for example: "I always felt like my body was wrong and in need of change. I was never the right size and I was always comparing myself to others. I never felt like I was good enough, and I was always trying to change myself."

Alina identifies an overarching feeling that her body is not what it is expected to be, either by herself or those around her. The anxiety Alina describes around her body not being what she thinks it should be is a common driver of body hatred.

Body size is often a primary concern for people who hate their bodies, but sometimes there is a specific body part or proportion that causes suffering. Lily is a mother and lawyer who, when she began her recovery from body hatred, described feeling as though her body proportions were wrong. And despite cognitively understanding feminist theory on body hatred, she continued to see and feel her body as wrong. She was regularly exposed to ideas about the impact of the current iteration of patriarchy on women's relationships with their bodies, but she still viewed her own body as the problem instead of the cultural conditioning that caused her to see her body in certain ways. Lily's story highlights that cognitive understanding alone is often not enough to help us feel calm about our bodies. While she could understand the social influences that make people hate their bodies, she couldn't get over her sense that her own body was "out of proportion."

You too might cognitively understand the function of body hatred in your life—where it comes from, the systems of oppression that fuel it—but that understanding is not enough to change how you feel. For Lily, her recovery did involve sorting through the cultural influences that had led her to the place she was, but more than that, it required an emotional and spiritual journey of learning who she really is, why she is here, and how to relate to her own body differently.

Feeling the Need to Control Your Body

Paradoxically, the feeling of accomplishment when your body is controlled in terms of weight, shape, and appearance can make overcoming body hatred challenging, because that feeling is so often followed by feelings of failure and shame when the regimen cannot be maintained or when your body does not respond to dieting, exercise, or other overt change attempts. Attempts to control the body are hard to change because often they work in the short term, but they can fuel body hatred in the long term, leading to a vicious cycle. It's also true that over time, your body might begin to resist change due to the metabolic adjustments it makes in response to inadequate nutrition, lack of rest, or overexercise. This vicious cycle can lead to an experience of crisis when your body isn't responding to attempts to change it the way it used to, and yet you feel that your body *still needs* to change.

For example, Maria is active and enjoys bicycling regularly. Her body appears to be what many would describe as "fit," but she still feels compelled to monitor her body. "I look at myself in the mirror every day and I pinch myself every day to see how fat I am and how much I need to change my eating." Maria illustrates how pervasive body anxiety can be—no matter her fitness level or body shape, she feels the need to constantly adjust her eating to control her body. This vigilance serves as the focus for her day. And it's been this way for so long that Maria struggles to imagine what her life might be like without it.

Feeling Disconnected from Your Body

At the beginning of recovery from body hatred, usually there is a sense of disconnection from your body and internal cues such as hunger, fullness, and even physical pain. It's not uncommon for people to become aware of long-standing physical needs (for example, back pain) when recovery begins, because the body has for so long been disconnected from the mind. Rather than *feeling* your body, body hatred has you *thinking about* your body.

For Julia, disconnection from her body had roots in inaccurate and inadequate emotional attunement from adults and caregivers. Julia grew up in a chaotic household and, as a result, felt very anxious. For most of her life people commented on how confident she was, yet rarely asked about how she might be feeling. She states, "And that created a disconnect. I felt like my body was the part of me that was holding all that anxiety, like I'm watching myself from the outside. It didn't feel like the same as my mind. From a young age, I can remember feeling dissociated from my body." Ultimately, her body was where she felt the anxiety she did not know how to cope with. Under her anxiety ran deep emotions and reactions to the chaos around her, but instead of feeling those emotions and reactions, she learned to hate her body. She substituted grieving the state of her body for grieving the breakdown of her family. This eventually led to more pervasive body hatred and further disconnection from her body and feelings.

Disconnecting from our bodies is adaptive; it is a way we cope with emotions or experiences where we did not get adequate support. Like Julia, if we did not receive enough guidance in emotional awareness from our families or caretakers, we might learn to disconnect from our bodies—which register what we feel even when our minds do not—as a way to cope with overwhelming feelings.

Sarah remembered starting dieting at eight years old and going on and off diets well into her adulthood. She explained the cycle she endured before recovery:

> I went through phases that are so typical—starting a diet, losing a little bit of weight, feeling out of control, going off the diet, gaining weight. I felt very disconnected from my body. I tried to ignore the problem, but it would come up when I had big family events, or when others started to diet and I would too.

For Sarah, the cycle of dieting and body hatred impacted her life by consuming emotional and mental energy, but also by disrupting her felt sense of her body.

Feeling disconnected from the body is a primary marker of body hatred. Rather than feeling the body and attending respectfully to body cues of hunger, fullness, and need for rest or movement, we miss cues altogether, or we end up pathologizing them, treating them as signals that we need too much and are wrong on a deep level. The feeling that the body is wrong leads to feeling that we ourselves and our needs are wrong.

Feeling Stressed about Your Body

People who suffer with body hatred usually feel incredible stress about their bodies that they can track even into early childhood. Sarah described the stress and sense of scrutiny she felt living in her body as a child thusly: "My body has always been under some sort of stress. I was never running around as a kid and not caring about my body like I think kids do." This sense of precariousness, as though the body needs to be managed and watched, creates a sense of tenuousness and stress in life. Additionally, self-consciousness about being witnessed by others, including family and medical providers, often creates an atmosphere of body stress and self-consciousness.

We learn to attune to our feelings and our bodies by example and by reflection. If, as children, we lived in an environment with people who did not know how to feel and cope with their emotions and, thus, couldn't help us tend our own, that often predisposes us to anxiety. From there, anxiety can easily turn into body anxiety—especially in a culture that is swamped in unrealistic body ideals already. We will talk more about this triangle—hard feelings turn into anxiety, which can lead to body hatred—as we go.

Feeling Protected by Privilege and Healthy Rebellion

Unfortunately, body hatred often coexists with eating disorders, disordered eating, or similar concerns. But there are some protective factors that can keep people from moving from body hatred to overt eating disorders. Privilege in all its forms often protects from more severe forms of suffering. One major example of body privilege is thin privilege, which is the social benefit of living in a body that conforms to some degree to idealized social standards. Healthy inner rebellion against family and cultural values can also support people in resisting body hatred. For example, Julia described rebelling against her mother's own body hatred by refusing to exercise like her mother did, which was more about atonement for eating than movement itself. Rebellion towards her mother's body hatred did not make Julia like her own body, but it supported her in creating a boundary between herself and values that she did not want to emulate. Cultivating rebellion is a necessary tool along the body peace journey, and glimpses of rebellion can often be seen at the beginning of the journey.

Which of these themes resonate for you? Have you had any of these experiences—thinking that your body is wrong, feeling the need to control it, feeling disconnected from it or stress about it? Conversely, are there any that feel strange to you? The idea that privilege or rebellion can be a protective factor masking body hatred seems strange to many.

Whatever comes up for you, take some time to journal about your thoughts now.

_____

_____

_____

_____

The Light at the End of the Tunnel

Deep down, maybe you know body hatred is an inner problem. It's also psychological, familial, and cultural. The all-encompassing nature of the problem can make it seem overwhelming to address—particularly because physical solutions, like dieting and exercise, are constantly being marketed as long-term solutions. But if a diet or new form of exercise were all you needed, you would have succeeded already. I'm here to say it's okay to feel overwhelmed by the magnitude of this problem, much of which stems from systems that are often out of our control (including the wellness, fitness, and beauty industries). But there is also a light at the end of the tunnel.

Here's what I know:

1. Body hatred is complex. We hate our bodies for a plethora of reasons that stem from impossible beauty standards; family beliefs around health, weight, and appearance; racial, sexual, and gender bias and discrimination; and our own internalized expectations of our bodies.

2. Overcoming body hatred will require you to feel your feelings and trust your body. Body hatred involves thoughts and projections onto our bodies that stem from beliefs we've absorbed from those around us: our bodies are too big, too small, too messy, too untamed, and so on. Underneath these projections and self-attacking thoughts are emotions, instincts, and intuitions that want to be felt.

3. Overcoming body hatred will ask you to protect yourself—internally and externally—by setting boundaries around how you think of yourself and how the world projects its problems onto you. These boundaries keep in what is life-giving and defend against what is life-taking.

4. Overcoming body hatred will help you feel more like yourself, because you will actually *feel* yourself from the inside out, rather than *thinking* about yourself from the top down.

5. Overcoming body hatred will make you more powerful, because all that energy you once used to hate your body can be channeled into meaningful work in the world: activities that are enlivening, relationships that feed you, and effective action around causes that are important to you.

Take another moment to consider and write down what these aims—feeling your feelings, trusting your body, becoming more powerful, living a life that truly nourishes—mean to you. Do they resonate for you? Do they feel challenging, even impossible? Anything you feel here is okay; the point is to recognize it and be curious about what's emerging.

_____

_____

_____

_____

Recovery as a Path to Soul

The work of overcoming body hatred is inner work; it's about relating to who we are and who we are becoming. It's an invitation to relax the hold of the dominant culture for a moment and go within. It may help to think of body hatred not as a problem to solve, but as a doorway to becoming more yourself. In other words, the journey through body hatred is one of recovery and individuation.

In Jungian psychology, *individuation* is the journey of settling into soul and living out the destiny you were born with, in relation to the times you're in. The analogy of an acorn growing into an oak tree may be useful. When the acorn is born, it is a little thing; it's not aware of the oak tree it will become. It becomes conscious of its destiny as an oak tree through living life. And it's not the acorn guiding the process; it's the unformed oak tree that beckons the acorn to grow, change, surrender in the face of all kinds of disruptions—which makes the oak tree unique, wise even. Similarly, your growth will occur through embracing your longings, moving through the griefs of life, and facing limitations and frustrations, all of which is a deeply human endeavor. Put another way, the acorn represents your small-s "self," the conscious self or ego. The capital-S "Self" is a larger vision for who you are and could become, akin to the oak tree acting as a blueprint, guiding the acorn through life. Another way to think of the capital-S Self is as the soul.

Right now, your relationship with your body might feel broken. Maybe you don't feel that you can be trusted in terms of your hunger, longings, or needs. Maybe your body is not the body you believe you should have. Maybe you feel a sense of urgency to simply solve your body problem so you can get on with your life. As you repair this feeling of brokenness, weaving together bits of self-trust through the choices, both big and small, that you make throughout your days, you will eventually notice that, yes, indeed there has been repair—and also that you have woven together an entirely new life. This life will likely be one that is rich, textured, and meaningful. This new life will be a departure from a life ruled by body hatred, which is often quite boring, guided by the same recurring thoughts and attempts to change your body that never really stick. Ultimately, by making peace with your body, you will be able to reside in your deep Self or soul.

There is a paradox here. On one hand, preoccupation with the body—how it looks, how much it weighs, how "healthy" it is—is a distraction from soul. When the body is the center of attention in our mental and emotional life, there tends to be little room for deeper questions and life experiences. However, the journey to recover from body hatred—which involves a different sort of contact with the body, contact with it just as it is—is itself a journey of deepening into soul. So preoccupation with the body and its state and perceived flaws is a hurdle—and also the path towards the deep Self, life calling, and connection with true values.

Through my own journey and work with people overcoming body hatred, I have found several themes that are present when people feel free of body hatred:

1. Engaging in life purpose: Often the work of overcoming body hatred leads to focusing on what we are passionate about and are motivated to change in the world. This emphasis on life calling and purpose is part of a deeper psychological change in which the ego is more consistently oriented toward the deep Self, or soul. Ultimately, we gain a sense of purpose in our work in the world.

2. Using one's voice: We learn to use our voices to set verbal boundaries, express ourselves, ask for what we need, disagree, and connect with others.

3. Gaining a sense of relief: Rather than feeling stuck in constant stress around our bodies, we feel a sense of breath and relief living in the bodies we have.

4. Making generational meaning: Through the work of recovering from body hatred, we come to understand that body hatred is larger than ourselves and that our problems with our bodies are not ours alone. Both the problem of hating our bodies and our work to make peace with our bodies extends beyond ourselves—to our children, families, and communities. Inner transformation is part of larger generational and ancestral healing.

5. Emanating rather than performing: When we are present in our bodies, we emanate a sense of who we are rather than acting or performing like a person in a body. Inhabiting our bodies fully keeps us connected to our genuine selves. We don't *try* to act a certain way; we naturally convey who we are.

The journey to overcome body hatred can lead to being in an attuned, respectful relationship with our bodies. This attuned relationship helps us live with purpose in our communities and the larger world.

Often people who have recovered from body hatred find that there is meaning in offering to others pieces of what they've learned from their own process. I've experienced this shift myself in my own journey of recovery. In the course of the journey, we develop the ability to live more in line with our values and to speak our needs or opinions more assertively, and we acquire a wide arsenal of coping strategies, internal and external, that we can model for others. Ultimately, overcoming body hatred is an initiatory process of becoming more in tune with our bodies, emotions, and soul longings, and even helping those around us do the same—a process you'll begin in this book.

True Hunger: Soul is Your Guide

True hunger is a term I use to describe the impulse from the deep self to individuate, to orient to soul and a more meaningful way of living our lives. Our true hungers pull us into the next right steps on our path.

Hunger, in this context, refers to what we long for—and as such, it changes with life seasons and developmental needs. During my active recovery from body hatred, my true hunger was to feel okay, to be able to sit still in a quiet moment without running away from myself. Years later, my true hunger was to birth and mother a child, which came to me in a flash, breaking through to consciousness one day. During the COVID-19 pandemic, my true hunger was to merely survive and learn something as a new mother. At other points in my life, my true hunger has been to deepen my marriage. Whatever the specific desire, true hunger is the calling from our souls—not from our waking, ego consciousness—and it speaks in longing, wanting, a gut-deep pull. It is not the same as striving, pushing, or "mind hunger," which is what we might think we want as a result of what we've been conditioned to believe we want or need. True or soul hunger is from the deep Self; it's purposeful and it wants to be heard.

We all have longings that come from deep within the soul. Longings that come from the soul level are organizing and healing. They lead us to make changes that can enable our most important life transformations. At the point in my life when I had the recurring fantasy of simply being okay in a simple moment, this fantasy was my true hunger. My life began to revolve around it and, thankfully, it led me onto the path that allowed me to become a therapist, teacher, writer, and mother. But there was no avoiding the mental and psychological work needed to get there.

Listening to true hunger is central to recovering from body hatred. It helps you remember that what you are deeply hungry for is something only contact with your own body and soul can satisfy. Soul hunger is a longing that is difficult to name, but when you feel it, you know it. You also know that no amount of body alteration, external achievement, or products can entirely fulfill this longing; it's an expression of inner hunger connected to the world's hunger. So often what we're hungry for, what we deeply long for, is an expression of a need of the collective. Longing for places for safe expression of our selves might be connected to a collective need for increased equity and inclusion that fosters safety for all bodies. Longing for relationships and connection might be related to a collective need for community and increased social contact in a technological world. Honoring our personal soul hungers can help us feel connected to the needs of the world—in which we're all deeply embedded.

When we disconnect from our bodies and physical hunger through suppression of appetite, being too "in our heads," or trying to manipulate our bodies to conform to socialized standards, we also disconnect from our inner wisdom and the deeper longings of our soul. Many people struggle with satisfying their true hunger. Many don't even know what it is. But in our day-to-day lives, we might grapple with the feeling that no matter how hard we work, how much we accomplish, it's still not enough. And while this feeling can be attributed to individual psychological patterns, family values, and social conditioning, this is also a pattern for people who struggle with body hatred—the same people who are cut off from knowing or satisfying their true hunger.

Ultimately, the work you are invited to do in this workbook is designed to support you in connecting to your true hunger as a pathway to embodiment and body peace.

EXERCISE:
Exploring True Hunger

What we long for in our lives can help us understand what we value, which is a compass for our lives. Body hatred often interferes in listening to these deeper values. Understanding what we long for is necessary to refocus attention from body hatred to building a life of meaning.

In the columns below, identify what you are hungry for physically, emotionally, spiritually, in relationships, in your work, and on a collective level. For example, in the physical column you might write "I am hungry for a more organized home so I can relax." For relationships, "I am hungry for more time with friends who are exploring new ideas and trying new things." For the collective, "I am hungry to see changes in social policy so our environment is protected."

Physically	Emotionally	Spiritually
Relationships	Work	Collectively

This practice of self-inquiry will help you begin to sense what is tugging at you. What you are hungry for is tied to what is important to you, which is often lost in the pain of body hatred.

Combining Insight and Practicality

This book is a combination of my experience and training in Jungian analysis, depth psychology and behavioral psychology, specifically dialectical behavior therapy (DBT) and cognitive behavior therapy (CBT). Depth psychology is concerned with meaning and purpose, while behavioral psychology is concerned with functioning and behavior change. These approaches are complementary and together serve as the foundation for this book.

Mindfulness and intuition are at the heart of both DBT and depth psychology, in different ways. Depth psychology emphasizes intuition, or a sense of a wise, guiding presence in our lives. We learn to orient to this presence through working with our dreams, our emotions, and our triggers, or complexes (explained in detail in chapter 2). Similarly, in DBT, there's a concept of "wise mind" that helps us move towards a "life worth living," in which we prioritize long-term values over short-term emotions. Coping with emotions effectively and becoming mindful of our inner experiences help us have enough inner control to avoid sabotaging what we want in our lives.

However, traditional DBT was designed for people who struggle to control their emotions and often feel out of control of their behavior as a result. And for many people who struggle with body hatred, more emotional control is not the missing piece—it's the other end of the spectrum that's lacking. We need less emotional control and more feeling; less rule-following and more spontaneity; less black-and-white thinking and more creativity. For the purposes of this book, I am using traditional DBT and depth psychology to support both ends of the spectrum: depth psychology to increase depth of feeling and inner curiosity, and DBT to provide practical coping strategies for both what you're facing now and what might arise as you access your true hunger and seek to change your life.

One of the biggest complaints I hear about DBT is how dry it can be. It's also common, in DBT treatment, for the central ideas of mindfulness and wise mind to be bypassed for the sake of coping skills. Similarly, in my depth psychology training, I often felt that behavioral or change-focused work to help people make practical use of the insights they were gaining was missing. So, in this book I utilize DBT as a kind of skills structure and depth psychology to deepen meaning. For example, in chapter 3, "Sorting the Mind and Heart," you'll learn the DBT skill of distinguishing between three states of mind: wise, emotional, and reasonable mind—a skill that's incredibly useful in organizing our inner experiences when body hatred is present and learning how to tap into true desires and soul hunger instead.

That said, people who struggle with body hatred are highly functional and emotionally intelligent people. They aren't necessarily in need of a larger arsenal of coping skills; what is missing is often a deeper connection with the body, values, and inner authority, along with systemic changes that support living peacefully in our bodies. This is why you'll find, alongside practical DBT-style interventions to get you doing things differently than you have been, a central thread of seeking insight into the deeper meaning that experiences like body hatred inevitably have. This approach comes from depth psychology, which emphasizes that while we might suffer with experiences like body hatred, there is meaning in this suffering. Then our suffering becomes more than purely pathological. Depth psychology treats our suffering as purposeful—even soulful—in the way that it can reflect and illuminate both our deep pain and our true hunger. The combination of these approaches supports recovery in a meaningful and useful way.

The discussion in the next chapter will cover the ways we become "dismembered," in a manner of speaking, by body hatred—pulled apart, separated from our bodies, made to hate the bodies we have—and how we might begin to "re-member" ourselves: to reconstitute ourselves through acceptance of the body and recognition of our true hunger, of who we really want to be and what we really want to do.

From there, the book is organized into three main topics: mind and emotions, body, and soul. In the third chapter, focused on working with your mind and emotions, you will learn how to work with the thoughts you have about your body, how to feel your emotions that fuel body hatred, and how to use these emotional impulses wisely. In the fourth chapter, focused on listening to your body, you will explore skills for feeling your body and listening to your body as a guide for your life. In the fifth chapter, focused on connecting to soul, you will learn what the experience of body hatred has to do with your soul longings, how to listen to your deep self through dreamwork, and how to use the knowledge you gain to deepen and enrich your life.

Weight Inclusivity and Body Liberation

This book also is guided by a weight-inclusive approach, honoring the awareness that body weight is informed by complex genetic, environmental, socioeconomic, and cultural factors. Anti-fatness is often rooted in histories of racial discrimination, specifically antiblackness (Strings 2019). As a result, body liberation movements ideally center black, indigenous, and people of color (BIPOC). While I am not BIPOC myself, my work with body hatred has made me aware of just how much anti-fatness is founded in racism. A focus on fatness—as opposed to thinness—has been largely omitted from general psychological literature until recently, with the advent of fat activism and body liberation movements. When we explore dwelling in and making peace with our bodies, weight and racial biases must necessarily be confronted. Work by BIPOC fat activists and researchers has much to offer regarding the systemic changes necessary for true body liberation.

To more specifically situate myself in this field, it's important to note that I am white, thin, cisgendered, and have benefited from white, thin, heteronormative privilege my entire life, along with many other privileges, including class. My struggles with food and my body were considered emotional and psychological in nature. Never did I receive suggestions to lower my weight or tips for changing my body in the way someone with a higher weight, considered "fat," would. As Cheryl Fuller (2017), a fat therapist, explains in her personal story, fat people are inundated with suggestions from thin people about how to change their bodies or tips and tricks that would make the fat person more like them. I was spared this dehumanizing experience. If you were not, I want to acknowledge that experience before our work begins. I also want to acknowledge that people of color and fat people receive drastically different treatment when seeking medical and psychological help (Phelan et al. 2015).

I mention weight inclusivity now mostly to clarify that it is not the focus of this book to highlight weight changes as a path towards body peace. Rather, I am guiding you to consider the cultural, emotional, and spiritual path of body peace—which is inevitably one of finding peace in your body, no matter which body it happens to be, and making peace with the fact that all bodies will inevitably change. I'll also note that while this book is not focused on fatness specifically, there is a pervasive fear of fatness culturally, one that often comes in the guise of health concerns for people as they are learning to live in their bodies peacefully. I want to make it clear now, at the outset of our work together, that fear of and stigma against fatness is a deep-rooted cultural issue that we are attempting to halt and unwind here, rather than continue to perpetrate.

Now that you've been introduced to the theoretical foundations that underlie this book, let's begin exploring some of the insights DBT has to offer.

Considering the "Kernel of Wisdom"

Before we choose to change a pattern in our lives, it's important to be clear on what might be sacrificed in change—and what change might make possible. In DBT, we consider that every problem behavior has a "kernel of wisdom" within it, even if it causes us suffering. This exercise is to help you consider the role of body hatred in your life. In what ways does body hatred interfere in living the life you want? And in what ways might body hatred be protective or wise? How can you recognize the kernels of wisdom present in your behavior and take them with you even as you seek to change?

Some of the questions in this exercise may provoke intense feelings. Do your best to be with them while staying mindful of your needs.

BENEFITS ASSESSMENT:
Finding the Kernel of Wisdom

1. Imagine a moment in the last week when you felt deep in body criticism. What were you feeling? What were you thinking?

    _____

    _____

2. What was happening earlier in the day that might have prompted this experience of body criticism? Was there anything stressful, emotionally unsatisfying, or hurtful that happened?

    _____

    _____

3. Consider what was happening that day. What might criticizing your body have been doing for you? In other words, was criticizing your body serving a purpose of some kind?

    _____

    _____

4. Taking an even wider lens, what might hating your body be doing for you? Does it protect you from anything? Does it allow you to avoid anything? Does it help you to connect to people?

    _____

    _____

    _____

    _____

CONSEQUENCES ASSESSMENT:
Assess the Sacrifice

1. In what ways does body hatred interfere in your life? Consider work, relationships, spirituality, family, life goals, areas of passion and activism, and anything else that is meaningful to you.

_____

_____

_____

_____

_____

_____

2. More specifically, in what ways does body hatred interfere in living the life you feel called to live?

_____

_____

_____

_____

_____

_____

Pulling It Together

1. If you could change these patterns, would it be worth the effort?

    _____

    _____

    _____

    _____

2. What would you do with your life if you weren't suffering with body hatred?

    _____

    _____

    _____

    _____

    _____

3. Take a moment to imagine yourself free from body hatred. What do you imagine?

    _____

    _____

    _____

    _____

    _____

In the course of this exploration, some questions might have come up about body hatred and about what you might need to do as you confront and work with it. Let's take a moment to consider them now.

Questions To Begin

Do I have to love my body before I can overcome hating my body? This is an understandable question to face and to feel ambivalent about. It's likely many of us have a complicated relationship with the idea of "self-love" despite encountering it as an often-touted solution to complex inner experiences. But the opposite of body hatred is not body love. When body hatred is healed, the result is *embodiment*—living in one's body with attunement and respect. We will discuss attunement in detail in the next chapter, but for now, it refers to sensing and being in tune with ourselves.

Respectfully living in your body is more realistic than the pressure to "love your body" when you don't actually love your body—a form of toxic positivity especially common now. The reality is that ambivalence about our bodies is normal and natural. Our bodies exist to experience a life well-lived, and then they die—and we can be grateful for them without liking what they look like at all phases of our lives.

Ultimately, "self-love" can be a form of body positivity, which is often simply an attempt to cognitively change the ways we think about our bodies—sometimes successful, sometimes not. It's not the same as feeling *at ease* with our bodies, which goes deeper than body positivity. Feeling at ease with our bodies—being embodied—is the ability to live in our own skin and take care of ourselves. It's the ability to tolerate the pleasures and discomfort in our bodies as these feelings arise.

As your journey continues, you'll likely find that viewing your body with neutrality, rather than with disgust or forced love, is a byproduct of living respectfully in your body. Ultimately, attempting to put on rose-colored glasses instead of hate-colored ones is simply swapping one way of viewing for another. What you're looking for instead is a new relationship with your body and self that's based in relationality—feeling, sensing, understanding, and accurate responding.

Is wanting to change my body while I do this work a bad thing? Wanting your body to be or look or function in a way it doesn't right now is part of what you will come to terms with on this journey to overcome body hatred. It is not wrong or bad to want to change your body; in fact, of course you do! Wanting to change your body is expected in the dominant North American culture (which is where I'm writing from). All day every day, we are inundated with media and messages that sell an image of what our bodies could or should look like. Accepting the presence of this desire, and the forces that shape and perpetuate it, is the first step. And the next step is asking, what if it could stop there? What if I could want to change my body *and* get on with my life? What if I could want to change my body *and* I don't let this make me hate my body? In such moments, you are holding the tension between wanting your body to change and not letting that turn into body hatred—and holding that tension gently.

Is trying to change my body while I do this work going to interfere in overcoming body hatred? Actively trying to change our bodies is not something any of us give up easily. And the reality is we will always be in some form of communication with our bodies about how much movement they want, how much they want and need to eat, about our bodies' needs as they change—whether we are pregnant or menopausal, recovering from an illness or grief, celebrating a new love, or any number of other experiences. The invitation for the duration of this book is to simply consider what might be possible if attempts to change your body were given less energy. At the same time, I trust you with your body and knowing what is right for you in any given season of life.

Can I continue to exercise while recovering from body hatred? Movement that is pleasurable, fun, and sustainable is a human need. However, many people who struggle with hating their bodies need to learn how to move their bodies in ways that feel good and don't hurt them in some way. So yes, movement is encouraged, particularly if it feels joyful and life-giving, but if it's time to rest after a long time of pushing your body, then that is also welcome. Use your best judgment to determine what it is you truly need right now, and do your best to give yourself that as you continue on this journey.

Words of Hope

Sometimes when I'm sitting on the couch with my daughter watching an episode of *Cocomelon* for the 157th time, I am startled to notice that I am okay. I can sit with myself, with my daughter, and I'm not jumping out of my skin concocting the next food restriction plan in my head or feeling an urgent need for change. I can be with myself, in myself, and take a deep breath.

I am endlessly grateful that my relationship with my body is relatively peaceful. This peace is born out of the intersection of my many, many privileges. It is also born out of unearthing swallowed-whole messaging about my body, feeling my body from the inside out, and listening to my emotions and intuitions as guides to my soul.

People often begin to question their body hatred when their desperate attempts to change or maintain their bodies begin to fail. Maybe you're too tired to continue doing what you've been doing and know you need a different way long-term. I celebrate this moment of exhaustion, because that's when you can open to a different way of being. I welcome you and honor how much you've likely already done to feel better.

As a final exercise for this beginning chapter, I invite you to start to think about what it would feel like to truly accept your body as it is.

EXERCISE:
Radical Acceptance

Radical acceptance is a coping skill taught in DBT focused on accepting reality as it is to reduce unnecessary suffering. By radically accepting reality, we gain choices for what to do with reality. But if we are fighting reality (in this case, the reality of our bodies as they are today) then we stay stuck, arguing with what is rather than making room for "What next?"

Overcoming body hatred will require accepting the reality of your body. The full journey is nuanced, but let's consider a possible end result by radically accepting your body as it is, simply to get some insight on why this work might be worth it. Use the following exercise to lead you through the process and journal what you notice along the way.

1. Take a couple deep breaths, in and out. Allow yourself to settle into the present moment.

2. Notice how you feel towards your body in this moment. What emotions do you notice? What thoughts are you having about your body?

    _____

    _____

    _____

3. How does your body feel in this moment? What sensations do you notice: numbness, tightness, tingling? If noticing your body sensations is new to you, ask your body where it is feeling something and imagine sending your breath to that spot for a moment.

    _____

    _____

4. Now imagine casting a wide, invisible circle around your body. Imagine that this circle can hold everything. Allow it to hold your thoughts and feelings about your body, your body's sensations, and your body just as it is right now.

5. Take a breath and imagine softening your heart to accept this circle and what is inside. Imagine not resisting the reality of your body and how you feel about your body.

6. Pause to consider:

    •   What do you feel as you allow your body to be as it is?

    _____

    _____

    •   What does your body feel as it is allowed to be as it is?

    _____

    _____

    •   What is sacrificed by fighting with your body?

    _____

    _____

    •   What is accomplished by fighting with your body?

    _____

    _____

    •   What might be possible if your body was not a site of anger and frustration, but rather your place to reside within for the course of your life?

    _____

    _____

    _____

7. When you feel complete with this practice, close with three deep breaths.

CHAPTER 2

Hating the Bodies We Have and Becoming Who We Are

When we hate our bodies, our bodies feel like a burden, something separate from ourselves. The feeling that "My body isn't really 'me'" can be thought of as a state of dismemberment. Dismemberment, in its literal form, is a common theme in mythology, such as the myths of Dionysus, Osiris, and Medusa. The same stories often entail transformation and initiation through re-membering—the process of pulling the pieces of one's body together into a new, different whole. This process is part of the journey you'll take to making peace with your body: moving from a state of dismemberment to re-membering yourself and discovering a larger sense of purpose for your life. This chapter is focused on helping you understand why we get dismembered, pulled apart, from our bodies, while the following chapters focus on re-membering or coming back into ourselves as whole beings.

A Normative Discontent: Dieting and Fat Phobia

For most of my life, there were only a few people I knew who did not verbally disparage their bodies or restrict food as a regular practice to change their bodies. Body hatred can affect anyone no matter their gender, race, sexual orientation, or ability. Body hatred and attempts at body change, including weight loss, are pervasive, even when they appear in the guise of detoxing or clean eating, as is the case in the contemporary wellness industry.

In 1984, researchers coined the phrase "normative discontent" to describe subclinical body hatred (Rodin et al. 1984) that includes dieting and body preoccupation. While subclinical body hatred lies along the spectrum of eating disorders and disordered eating, normative discontent and the suffering it engenders is rarely addressed in psychological research. Body hatred continues to be so *normal* that even in a therapy setting, it's not uncommon for a therapist to support weight loss or "fitness" efforts rather than explore the deeper motivations for this attitude.

In other words, normative discontent is body hatred that is so familiar it's rarely named. Perhaps the worst part of body hatred is the private moments of stress and struggle and deep isolation that accompany feeling not at home in your own skin. The moments of feeling not okay, anxious, worried, and out of place due to feelings about your body are the signifiers of body stress. They're not to be minimized; the amount of psychic and emotional energy that is given to body hatred is immense.

It's also true that despite evidence about the poor health outcomes and failure rates of dieting, people continue to diet—to engage in one of the most common responses to normative body discontent. "Dieting" as a term has gone out of vogue, replaced by more socially acceptable terms like intermittent fasting, clean eating, low-carb diets, high-carb diets, and all the forms of food restriction that come in and out of cultural awareness. But often, at the center of this cultural obsession with diet is not a drive toward true health but an abhorrence of fat and a drive toward control, perfection, and discipline (Strings 2019). A uniting factor within any weight loss campaign is the foundational moralizing of "thinness" over "fatness" despite attempts to present efforts to be thin as health-motivated.

What have your own experiences been with the ongoing pressure that accompanies normative body discontent? What have the labels "thin" and "fat" meant to you, for instance? Have you felt the urges toward control and perfection that drive diet or "health" culture? How have they manifested in your life?

_____

_____

_____

_____

_____

_____

For most of us, "thin" and "fat" generate psychological images imbued with particular meaning and psychic energy, associated with physical body characteristics. In America, the fear of fatness that motivates compulsive dieting, with compulsive eating (bingeing) as dieting's ever-present ally, is bound up with objectification of oppressed bodies, economic systems operating within our medical and advertising industries, and internalized fantasies of fatness and thinness (Farrell 2011). But body size and weight are influenced by a host of factors, including genetics, social stigma, trauma, and family history, to name a few. Since we are largely not in control of our body weight and size, it is a psychological journey to come to peace with the bodies we have been given, which rarely conform to internalized cultural ideals.

Why Do We Hate Our Bodies?

The reasons we end up hating our bodies are deeply personal and cultural. This section is not an exhaustive explanation of why we hate our bodies, but offers an overview of common themes associated with body hatred: experiences of trauma, experiences of objectification, invalidation of our feelings and needs by those around us, and the fat phobia and weight bias rampant in many cultures and families. (As noted in the first chapter, since this workbook is focused on body hatred related to body size and appearance, it does not include explanations for the racial, gender-based, or ability-related aspects of body hatred. The resources section at the end of this book offers guidance on these issues, if you need it.)

From "Big-T" Trauma to "Little-t" Trauma

If we are suffering with body hatred, it is likely that we suffered a disruption with our body, ranging in intensity from traumatic to subtle and mundane. The traumatic end of the spectrum includes sexual assault, physical violation, and illness. Such events can be thought of as "Big T" trauma. An experience of acute violation can set in motion the need to distance ourselves from our bodies and emotions. Without adequate support, a traumatic experience can lead to a lifetime of body disconnection and body hatred.

On the more mundane side of the spectrum we find "normal" body objectification and hyperfocus on our body's appearance by others—the daily experiences of being exposed to judgments about bodies or expectations others have of our bodies and what they should look like, do, or accomplish. Such experiences can be thought of as "little-t" trauma. It may seem strange to think of everyday experiences as potentially traumatic, but ongoing experiences of body objectification can create self-consciousness and disrupt internal awareness (Fredrickson and Roberts 1997). In other words, it's distracting to be aware we are being watched, and we can absorb that awareness, come to closely watch and judge ourselves, and feel alienated from our own bodies as a result.

Objectification and the Body

Feminist scholars pioneered our understanding of the impact sexual objectification of women can have on their psychological health and sense of self. While the focus has often been on women's experiences, objectification—when a person is seen and treated as an object, with certain parts of their bodies or bodily processes prioritized over their full selfhood or humanity (Bartky 1990; Nussbaum 1995)—affects all genders and bodies. When a person is objectified, their body and personhood are separated; they are reduced to their appearance and silenced as an autonomous figure with agency and control of their own choices (Langton 2009). In other words, they are seen not as a person, with their own desires and the capacity for independent action, but as an object, there to be seen by and to satisfy others.

This understanding has led to more research on self-objectification—the process by which people come to view themselves as objects because of how they are seen by others or society. Self-objectification can have serious psychological implications, ranging from heightened depression and anxiety to lowered confidence in cognitive functioning (Gay and Castano 2010; Grabe and Hyde 2009). Objectification and self-objectification also reduce awareness of internal feelings, leading to a tendency to think about the body more than feeling or sensing the body, which correlates with a plethora of mental health risks, including eating disorders (Fredrickson and Roberts 1997).

Do you have a memory of feeling objectified—a moment when your body was the focus of others' perceptions or behaviors, rather than your thoughts, feelings, or actions? Were these isolated instances, or do they represent a lifetime pattern? How did this experience, whatever it happened to be, impact your relationship with your body?

_____

_____

_____

_____

_____

Relational Misattunement: Early Care and Body Hatred

Another significant disrupter of body peace is when we don't receive adequate attunement from our culture, families, and caregivers when we are young. Attunement is the "kinesthetic and emotional sensing of others" and essentially helps us feel understood (Erskine 1998). Put simply, when another person is attuned to us, we feel that our emotions are being recognized and understood by them. This feeling of being met helps us settle into ourselves and feel our feelings and physical sensations without running away. If, as many people experience, we are *not* met—if our emotions and needs are invalidated, rejected or dismissed, whether in dramatic or subtle ways—then we don't learn how to settle into our bodies, where our feelings reside.

For example, imagine you just finished your lunch and you still felt hungry. Imagine your internal response if someone said: "You're still hungry, let's find a snack to hold you over until dinner," versus "You can't still be hungry; you just ate lunch." This is a very simple example, but the first statement is one of validation and attunement to physical need—you're hungry—rather than minimizing or dismissing your experience. Repeated incidences of the kind of invalidation represented by the second statement can create an internal disconnect between the feelings you have and your ability to feel them, to meet the needs they point toward, and move on. This is a form of dismembering.

Lack of validation is one reason why body hatred is often intergenerational; people who are disconnected from their bodies through experiences of objectification, invalidation, or trauma can have a hard time helping others connect to their bodies. As we discussed in the first chapter, body hatred often includes being disconnected from our body and our internal cues, including hunger, fullness, and even physical pain, and this disconnect prevents us from knowing what we need. If we can't feel what we need, then we often turn to external rules (such as a diet) to tell us how to take care of our bodies. Lack of accurate emotional attunement from our caregivers can keep us from developing the inner attunement to our own bodies and emotions that validating care encourages. I'm focusing on caregivers, but similar issues can stem from cultural disintegration—such as difficulty feeling at home anywhere, even in our own bodies, because of a deep disconnection from land, place, and cultural rituals and ceremonies that situate us within the wider web of nature, the unseen, and our ancestors.

How did people react to your emotions when you were growing up? When you were scared, anxious, angry, or sad, what generally happened? Do you have memories of being comforted and soothed?

_____

_____

_____

_____

_____

How did people react to your physical needs when you were growing up? When you were hungry, hurt, or tired, what generally happened?

_____

_____

_____

_____

How do you feel these experiences influenced your relationship with your body? Did they help you feel at ease, stressed, or disconnected from your body?

_____

_____

_____

_____

Fat Phobia and Weight Bias

It is impossible to talk about the journey to body peace without talking about the lurking shadow of fat phobia. Fear of fatness is a primary hurdle on the journey to feeling at peace with our bodies. Fatness is not only a literal experience of adipose body tissue, but an emotional and symbolic image in our minds. Fatness is often freighted with certain fantasies; it's often used to signify laziness, immorality, lack of control, and dirtiness (Gutwill 2018). Thinness, on the other hand, is often associated with discipline, cleanliness, and being in control and represents a white, Protestant ideal (Strings 2019; Bordo 2003). Much has been written on the drive for thinness and beauty, yet relatively little about how the fear of fatness can interfere with body peace. It's vital to understand fatness and fear of fatness as primary hindrances to embodiment and how the stigmas and discrimination associated with fatness are so easy for us to internalize.

I want to clarify that I use the term *fat* not as a term of pathology but as a descriptive one—and to reclaim it from a fat-phobic culture. I also use this word to emphasize and highlight the emotional reactions it elicits. The word "fat" carries deep meaning beyond the physical body, including very real discrimination toward people who are fat. Fatness carries such potent projections that we are socialized to fear it and our own bodies as a result. But ultimately, both fatness and thinness are symbolic and literal. What we most repress and fear will, paradoxically, carry insight for our healing. Fear of fatness is no different. Working with our projections and ideas of it helps us understand ourselves, our fears, and our needs.

To illustrate this idea, here are some examples of what I hear in therapy sessions from people who are recovering from body hatred. When I ask them what scares them about the idea of listening to their bodies, they reply with comments like, "I'll never stop eating," or "I'll be too much," or "I'll get fat (or fatter)," or "I'll take up too much space," or "I won't be able to fit in." When we sit with them long enough, these fears often reveal deeper layers of concern that include taking up space, having a sense of agency, using our voice, and taking healthy risks. They can reveal grief, longing, wanting things to be different than they are—and the body bears the burden of these longings. Often when we are working with what living in our bodies really means, we hit up against core fears of fatness, what it symbolizes, and what it is masking.

EXERCISE:
Fear and Change Statements

Mark which statements you feel to be true about following your body's cues:

☐ If I listen to my body, I'll never stop eating.

☐ If I listen to my body, I'll never get up again.

☐ If I listen to my body, I won't be able to stand how much I'll change—I might get fat, I might gain weight, I might gain more weight.

☐ If I listen to my body, I'll be out of control.

☐ If I listen to my body, I won't ever fit in my clothes again.

☐ If I listen to my body, my body will change, and I won't be accepted.

☐ Other: If I listen to my body, _____

   _____.

☐ Other: If I listen to my body, _____

   _____.

☐ Other: If I listen to my body, _____

   _____.

Again, typically these fears are from messages and ideas you might have picked up from your family or from the culture—especially the idea that fatness means a certain kind of messiness, laziness, and being out of control. Yet when we confront these fears and understand that fear of fatness is largely based on cultural and social conditioning, we can say things like: "I eat what I desire and I am connected to my body's cues." We can say, "I use my voice and take up the perfect amount of space for my body and soul," Or we can say, "I am willing to be seen for who I am and the gifts I offer." On the other side of fat phobia is an embodied presence of self-trust and a sense you deserve to be in this world, rather than needing to hide and shrink from it.

Take a moment to reframe the statements you marked above about your fear of change into affirming statements that consider the positive, generative possibilities on the other side of change. For example: *If I listen to my body, I'll never stop eating* could transform into *If I listen to my body, I might feel nourished and satisfied.*

☐ If I listen to my body, I'll never stop eating. Or, if I listen to my body when it comes to food, I might

_____ .

☐ If I listen to my body, I'll never exercise again. Or, if I listen to my body around movement I might

_____ .

☐ If I listen to my body, I won't be able to stand how much I'll change—I might get fat, I might gain weight, I might gain more weight. Or, if I listen to my body around its size and shape I might

_____ .

☐ If I listen to my body, I'll be out of control. Or, if I listen to my body I might

_____ .

☐ If I listen to my body, I won't ever fit in my clothes again. Or, if I listen to my body my relationships to my clothing might

_____ .

☐ If I listen to my body, I won't be accepted for how much my body will change. Or, if I listen to my body my relationships might

_____ .

☐ Other: If I listen to my body, _____

_____ .

Learning to listen to our bodies requires listening for cues of hunger, fullness, or needs for rest or movement. Fat phobia often expresses itself as: "If I listen to my body, I will be out of control" → "If I am out of control, I will be unhealthy" → "If I'm unhealthy, I will be fat" → "If I'm fat, I'll need to be in control"... and the cycle continues. But the body and mind inevitably rebel against restriction, especially when it's in the service of punishment, of restraining aspects of ourselves we've deemed "bad" or "wrong." Paradoxically, overcontrol can lead to undercontrol, just as dieting inevitably leads to overeating. In therapy, we never find bingeing without restriction— and rather than focusing on curbing bingeing, if overeating is a concern, we start with assessing why and where the restriction is happening.

Fear of fatness creates a fear of the body and all that the body entails, a fear of our body's hungers, desires, and needs that are bound with instincts and the chthonic realm of life—the realm of being earthy or messily human; the realm related to the underworld or unconscious— what we are not in control of in ourselves. Coming into relationship with our bodies often means confronting fears of fatness, hunger, fullness, and desire.

Preoccupation with the body and food can also be seen through the lens of somatic trauma psychology, the branch of psychology that deals with the bodily responses we have to trauma in addition to cognitive and emotional ones. The somatic trauma tradition posits that body hatred creates protective dissociative states, states in which we're separated from threatening emotions, needs, and urges, which is another way we are dismembered. Fear of fatness fuels this dissociation, masking the fear we have of our deeper sensations and feelings, particularly rage, longing, and creative impulse.

With all this in mind, consider: what is your association with the word "fat" in particular? Is it positive, negative, or neutral? Where did these associations come from—school, family, friends, media, or somewhere else? And how have they affected you?

Sacred Symptoms: Echidna and Archetypal Healing

Depth psychology holds that we are made up of complexes, which are largely out of our conscious control. A *complex*, in depth psychology, is an emotionally charged cluster of thoughts, feelings, and memories organized around an archetypal core. *Archetypes* are deep energetic patterns in the psyche that we all experience in some form or another and that are reflected in the cultures and stories we grow up with. These archetypes appear in culture as mythological figures and gods and goddesses—that is, as *archetypal images*. Put another way, archetypes are the deep energetic riverbeds that underlie cultural and psychological life. Archetypal images are distinct from archetypes themselves; they're how archetypes are represented in cultures and are culturally relative.

You know you're in a complex if you feel in the grip of an emotion that isn't fully matching external reality. When we feel "triggered," that usually means a complex has been activated; we react not to what is happening in the moment, but as though we are in some older, past experience we've had. For example, you might have heard about a "mother or father complex," which is often used to describe why we might react to the world, relationships, or our inner states in ways our parents do or did. The center of a mother or father complex is the archetypal mother or father—the essence of *mother* and *father* that exists throughout time and across cultures. The idea is that our complexes are not solely informed by our literal parents, but rather from the deep, unconscious archetypes that then interact with the people who parent us (which can be all kinds of people including teachers, bosses, siblings, and institutions even), creating a web of experiences and memories.

Complexes are not positive or negative, although they can support or interfere in the way we would ideally want to live our lives. The image I use is that of internal roots, like the bloodstreams in our bodies, that process and circulate what we take in, creating what we need to grow the bones, muscles, and tissues of our physical body, according to an organizing force that is patterned, not random, underneath it all. So we are made up of complexes, but we are also capable of bringing them to consciousness so they are not lived out unconsciously, which can be problematic—for example, with inherited biases or prejudices. Body hatred is such a complex. Depth psychology holds that by becoming mindful of our complexes, we can learn about ourselves and what activates us—and that learning to relate to the central archetype of a complex is one way to disengage from the complex itself and develop a relationship with the sacred aspect of our symptoms.

Here is an example. When I was working on a research paper focused on the cultural dieting complex that propels "diet culture," I received this dream: *I see a woman become a larger-than-life sea creature/serpent. She takes a huge bite out of a large snake and I am shocked by her ability to bite and eat so ravenously and forcefully. She is dripping blood as she eats.*

The next day I looked at a book on Greek mythology for my research. I opened the book directly to a picture of the goddess Echidna. The picture showed a huge half-snake, half-woman figure just like the one in my dream. I had never heard of Echidna before this synchronistic moment. She is the cave-dwelling mother of monsters such as Kerberos, the Sphinx, and the Hydra of Lerna. Kerenyi (1951) describes Echidna thusly: "In half her body she was a beautiful-cheeked, bright-eyed young woman; in the other half she was a terrible, huge snake, thrashing about in the hollows of divine Earth and devouring her victims raw." She lives far away from the gods and mortals, inside the Earth, where she was placed by the gods. Echidna is mythically and psychologically marginalized. She is also ruthlessly hungry, as imagined through her ability to devour her victims raw.

My dream reverberated throughout the days that followed. What surprised me was not only the vividness of the images, but also the immense power of this creature that could eat a huge snake raw. There was an energetic potency to this figure. I began to envision Echidna as a natural psychological ally to a dieting preoccupation that emphasizes restraint of appetite, body, and feeling. She knows marginalization, she knows the power of her hunger, and she is fertile with all manner of creatures. This is the guiding archetype of true hunger—hunger is powerful, fierce, and fertile. Insisting on her hunger over control, embodying flesh to her edges rather than succumbing to a frail and too-tight frame, Echidna is an archetype that motivates the psyche to resist pressures to be thin at all costs, insisting on allegiance to deeper values.

Echidna can be imagined as the unconscious saboteur to our desperate cultural obsession with dieting and thinness. She holds medicine we need when we're stuck in oppressive systems. While her hunger might be terrifying, it challenges us to find the courage to be fierce and powerful when facing what is terrifying in ourselves: our deep, true hunger and emotions. The paradox of healing is that the symptom of dieting—fueled by its own trauma of oppression and dictates to fit into a narrow and ultimately impossible bodily aesthetic of "perpetually thin, toned, and in control"—contains its own medicine of rage, power, and embodiment, allowing us to reject what starves and suffocates us. Relating to Echidna psychologically is the work of body hatred recovery—we relate to our ability to set boundaries, protect our values, eat well, create, and unapologetically embody ourselves.

How does the image of Echidna strike you? Does it feel empowering, or frightening, or perhaps a bit of both? Or perhaps it's hard to know what you feel, or it doesn't feel like anything yet. Take a moment to write down your thoughts.

_____

_____

_____

_____

_____

_____

_____

_____

In the following chapters you will explore relating to the parts of yourself Echidna represents—the wild, fierce, clear voices inside that can support moving from body hatred to body peace. For now, let's explore the ways you might have been dismembered and where re-membering is wanting to happen.

EXERCISE:
Reflecting on Your Early Body Story

Much of this chapter has focused on the ways we become disconnected from our bodies and emotions in early life. This next journaling exercise will support you in finding clarity on your own early body story. Take some time to reflect on what has informed your relationship to your body. (Note: Most people's body stories have moments of intensity, including traumatic experiences. If you want to go into this more charged material, do so with a trusted guide or therapist so as not to overwhelm your body and mind. If you are using this book on your own, it is okay to skip parts, or focus only on content that is tolerable to you.)

Identify the following moments in your early body history:

1.   What is your first memory of your body?

    _____

    _____

2.   Was there a moment you realized you had a body that was visible to others?

    _____

    _____

3.   Was there a moment or age or time period when your body stopped being the place you lived in and became something that needed to be managed?

    _____

    _____

4.   When was the first time your hunger came into question? Maybe someone commented on your body, your food choice, your appetite… Was there a moment when you noticed that what you ate mattered?

    _____

    _____

5.   When was the first time your enthusiasm or excitement was questioned? Can you remember when someone told you to "tone it down" or "rein it in"? What effect did this have on you?

_____

_____

_____

6.   Were you ever told your body was wrong in some way? If so, how did this impact you?

_____

_____

7.   Were you ever told your hunger was wrong in some way? If so, how did this impact you?

_____

_____

8.   How did people react to your emotions when you were growing up?

_____

_____

_____

9.   How did the people around you (family, close friends) feel about their bodies? What impact did this have on your relationship with your own body?

_____

_____

_____

We've addressed how pervasive and damaging certain patterns can be for our relationship with our bodies—patterns of being treated primarily as a body rather than a whole person (objectification), of not having our emotions reflected back to us (emotional misattunement and invalidation), and of fears of listening to our bodies (fat phobia). We've talked about how people associate fatness with ill health and being out of control and thinness with good health and being in control. This next exercise is to help you gain insight into your own relationship to listening to your body. What do you fear? What might be the benefits?

EXERCISE:
What Would It Be Like to Listen to Your Body Now?

Moving into an imaginal process: Imagine for a moment that you know how to listen to your body as a guide for how to move, eat, and rest. In this scenario, your body is your primary guide for when you eat and what you eat. Your body tells you when to move and how. Your body tells you when to rest.

What do you imagine happening? What is a normal day like? How do you feel, imagining listening to your body as a guide?

_____

_____

_____

_____

_____

_____

_____

_____

_____

_____

_____

CHAPTER 3

Sorting the Mind and Heart

A guiding myth that I like to use during the first steps of recovery from body hatred is the ancient Greek myth of Psyche and Eros. In the myth, mortal Psyche is so beautiful that people start worshiping her instead of the goddess of beauty, Aphrodite. Aphrodite becomes jealous and commands her son Eros, the god of love, to make Psyche fall in love with the worst creature he can find. However, Eros accidently pierces himself with his arrow containing the potion that incites love, and he himself falls in love with Psyche and makes her his wife in secret.

But Eros insists that Psyche can never look upon him in the light. When Psyche breaks this rule, Eros leaves her. Psyche seeks the help of Aphrodite to find him again. The goddess gives her four tasks, with the first one being the sorting of a pile of mixed seeds by daybreak— poppy, millet, lentils and more. This seems impossible, but tiny, humble ants come to Psyche's aid and by morning, the seeds are separated. Each subsequent task Psyche is given is just as impossible, yet Psyche is helped by forces beyond her control to complete each one. In the end, Aphrodite keeps her word, Psyche is reunited with her love, and they are married.

Psyche represents the human soul that is learning how to be in relation to larger, transpersonal forces, including love, beauty, and the divine. Her first task is the modest task of inner organization and discernment: the psychological work of separating our internal worlds, examining our thoughts, feelings, beliefs, and human life experiences. It's also what happens in psychotherapy—we sort through in order to understand and make the unconscious conscious by paying careful attention to our inner experiences, particularly the more troublesome parts.

The operative word here is *careful*—we care for our inner worlds, paying attention to the seeds we are sorting by shedding light on thoughts and feelings that we might wish we could simply ignore, but that have been waiting for attention. The gift of learning how to sort our inner psychological material is one that we carry forward through the rest of the journey, just as Psyche continues her journey towards Eros, the unification of human soul and divine love.

Skills of Mind and Heart

On the journey to recover from body hatred, we must sort through the jumble of conditioning and feelings we have internalized about our bodies. This is humbling work that helps us to see ourselves clearly from a grounded place. We need to discern which thoughts about our bodies are true and which ones are not; which thoughts and beliefs harm us and which ones support our becoming. Recovery from body hatred entails skills of mind and emotion, learning how to:

- Distinguish thoughts of body hatred from your true emotions; sort out what you think about your body from what you are feeling.

- Identify what you are feeling and understand how to respond compassionately and effectively to what you are feeling. Identify what the signals of emotion are saying to you by activating the inner "ants" carefully, paying attention to the particular feelings you experience as instincts guiding you towards a need, a longing, or something to express.

- Externalize what you have internalized, which means seeing how body hatred is largely influenced by outside forces (family, culture, media), so you can consistently put these influences back in their place, in the pile labeled "Cultural Conditioning that Made Me Hate My Body."

The exercises in this chapter are designed to support you in developing these skills. The practices are very much in the arena of behavioral psychology in that they encourage you to consider thoughts and feelings and evaluate them. But they are also useful in terms of their mythological significance, as they encourage attention to your inner world, including care for the bothersome thoughts and feelings you experience. Imagine the skills in this chapter, of learning to care for your psychological and emotional world, as Psyche being aided by the ants who carefully identify each seed in the overwhelming pile and put it in its right place, which is the foundation for reuniting body and soul.

Looking at the Pile of Seeds

This exercise is designed to help you consider your own metaphorical pile of seeds. Imagine your inner life—your thoughts, feelings, beliefs—as the seeds that Psyche must sort if she has any hope to be reunited with her love. By trusting your instincts, knowing you don't have to be perfect, begin to make your piles of seeds by completing a brain dump and noticing themes.

1. Set a timer for 10 minutes. Write—in brainstorm fashion, without censorship or judgement—all that's happening inside related to your current relationship with your body. What are you thinking about your body? What are you feeling towards your body? What are you worried about? What do you wish were true regarding your body and your relationship with your body? What do you know is true regarding your body? In recovering from body hatred, what do you hope happens in your life, your family, your work, or your community?

2. When the timer ends, read through your brainstorm answers. Using colored markers or pens, circle similar themes and topics. These might include judgments about your body, longings and desires, old messages and conditioning, and anxieties. You can also circle thoughts or feelings that are emotionally related—for example, all the thoughts that are related to anger, sadness, or excitement. Trust your instincts by clustering the thoughts and feelings from your pile in a way that makes sense and resonates with you.

3. Reflect on the dominant themes you circled. What is taking up the most space in your inner world? What is worrying you the most? Is there anything that surprised you while looking at all your thoughts and feelings about your body in this way?

_____

_____

_____

_____

_____

_____

_____

_____

_____

Clearing Internalized Messages

One of the reasons this internal sorting process is so important is that we internalize so much about how we feel about our bodies as young ones, from our culture and families. Imagine a little guppy floating in water, breathing and drinking in everything around her, day after day. That is what we are like as children, breathing in all that's around us, including beliefs and biases, other people's feelings about their bodies, and other people's beliefs about other people's bodies. It's a lot! What we learn about who we are, what acceptable behavior looks like, and how to live in our bodies from family, friends, and culture is called *imprinting*. It's done implicitly; we don't even have to be told explicitly what to believe because we breathe it in naturally, without defenses.

Because as children we do not have psychological protections in place that allow us to question what we are taught, as adults we must work to uncover what we "breathed in" in childhood that no longer makes sense for us—including beliefs about ourselves, our bodies, and how to be in the world. We often inherit beliefs around pleasure, boundaries, money, power, and responsibility (among many other values) that, when named, may have us wondering where in the world they came from. For instance, you might obey the belief "If I'm not controlling my body with exercise and dieting, other people will judge me" without consciously realizing that's the rule you're following. These unconscious dictates can lead to us feeling as though our lives aren't our own. And in some ways, they aren't. If we aren't questioning and looking at our unconscious motivations, then we tend to live out the desires of our caregivers, corporations, or other authority figures.

EXERCISE:
Clearing Out the Old

Complete the following prompts to identify outdated messages about your body and update them with ideas that better reflect the person you are today and want to become.

The Past

- What were you taught about how your body should appear? What were you taught about living in your body? *Growing up, I was taught my body should...*

_____

_____

_____

_____

- How did people around you feel about their bodies? How did your caregivers treat their bodies? *Growing up, people around me thought their bodies should...*

_____

_____

_____

_____

- How were you taught to take care of your body? *Taking care of my body meant...*

_____

_____

_____

_____

The Present

- How do you think your body should look now? *In my life now, I believe my body should appear...*

  _____

  _____

  _____

- How do people around you feel about their bodies? How do people around you talk about and treat their bodies? *People around me talk about and treat their bodies...*

  _____

  _____

  _____

  _____

- How do you take care of your body today? *Today, taking care of my body means...*

  _____

  _____

  _____

  _____

The Future

- How do you want your relationship with your body to feel? How do you want to live in your body? *I want to my relationship with my body to feel...*

  _____

  _____

  _____

- How do you want the people you're surrounded by to feel about and treat their bodies? *I want to be surrounded by people who treat their bodies...*

  _____

  _____

  _____

- How do you want to take care of your body that you don't already? *I want to take care of my body in new ways by...*

  _____

  _____

  _____

  _____

Sorting and Organizing

As you start to question internalized ideas about your body, you might start to notice how intertwined thoughts about your body are with how you feel, how intertwined longing to be part of a community or family is with desires for your body to be different, or how intertwined anger about your body is with thinking how much you want your body to change. Imagine these intersecting thoughts, emotions, and longings as the pile of seeds Psyche is tasked with sorting. The humble, focused ants help her complete what seems an insurmountable task. A relevant psychological skill uses the *three states of mind* concept from DBT. The three states of mind are *rational mind, emotion mind,* and *wise mind* (Linehan 2015). The goal of developing this skill is to be able to recognize when we are in each state of mind and eventually to land in wise mind more often than not. Wise mind is our center of intuition; it helps us synthesize what we feel emotionally with what we know rationally. Recognizing these three states of mind can help us move consciously between emotions, mental analysis, and our deeper wisdom. Using the three states of mind concept is a simple, effective way to organize our inner world, which can often feel so chaotic.

Rational Mind

Rational mind refers to thinking logically and objectively, relying on facts, reasoning, and analysis. In this state, we tend to be focused on problem-solving, using cognitive processes to make decisions based on evidence and reason. It is the "computer" part of ourselves. It helps us get through the day by completing tasks, organizing facts, and making decisions. We use rational mind when we make a grocery list, solve a problem at work, or find our way through a new city.

- *Strengths:* Rational mind is logical, solves problems, and sees patterns.

- *Weaknesses:* When unbalanced, rational mind can lead to life feeling hollow, meaningless, and disconnected.

Emotion Mind

Emotion mind is the feeling, sensing, and emotional part of ourselves. Feelings tell us what matters to us. Emotions are instinctually protective—without fear we would walk into traffic, without anger we wouldn't have boundaries, without love we wouldn't have social connection. Emotion mind puts color in our lives and highlights our values.

- *Strengths:* Emotion mind reacts quickly in emergencies, helps us love each other, protects us with fear and anger, and reveals meaning through joy, sadness, grief, excitement, etc. It helps us know what is we truly value.

- *Weaknesses:* When unbalanced, emotion mind can lead to impulsivity, pushing us to actions we may later regret. It can interfere in long-term desires if we don't temper it with emotional regulation skills.

Wise Mind

Wise mind blends both rational and emotion mind but is deeper than both of these. It is our intuition, our deep wisdom. Wise mind usually sounds like a voice of compassion, understanding, and moderation. When we are in wise mind, often we feel settled, like a "thud" of knowing or a jolt of insight that somehow simply feels true. People often report feeling wise mind in their bellies or hearts. Ultimately, if we can center ourselves in wise mind, we connect to our inner wisdom, feeling our emotions yet still allowing for rational thinking.

- *Strengths:* Wise mind centers us in a feeling of peace and knowing, even as we are experiencing an emotion. It helps us find deeper truth underneath body hatred and anxiety.

- *Weaknesses:* Too much focus on wise mind can lead to spiritual bypassing, which can be a way of avoiding (bypassing) more complex psychological issues, relational attachment wounds, or unresolved traumas (Welwood 2000).

EXERCISE:
Integrating Different Facets of Mind

Let's practice listening to the different facets of your mind you've just learned about—your rational perspective, your emotions, and the wise state of mind that integrates the two with your intuition and inner wisdom. Start by choosing a situation you've been chewing on. This could be a problem where you feel conflicted or a decision that you need to make—for example, addressing conflict with a friend or how to proceed with a tricky work situation. Then take a deep breath and ask yourself a question that encapsulates what you would like to know about this situation. You might ask, "How can I approach my friend about my feelings?" or "What's the next step for me in my career?"

Then move through each state of mind, writing down what comes to you naturally, starting with your rational self. Step back and observe the situation with clarity and objectivity. Take note of the facts, evidence, and practical considerations that come to mind. Next, shift gears to your emotional mind. Let your emotions speak their perspective and capture that perspective in writing, unfiltered. Finally, invite your wise mind to join the conversation. Listen closely to the whispers of your intuition and the guidance of your inner wisdom.

Situation: _____

My question about the situation: _____

Identify facts: What are the facts about this situation? What does my rational mind **think** of this situation?

_____

_____

_____

The answer to my question from my logical self: _____

_____

Identify feelings: What do I **feel** about this situation? What does the emotional part of me have to say about it? What have I not yet felt about the situation that I need to?

_____

_____

_____

The answer to my question from my emotional self: _____

_____

_____

Identify intuition: What does my **intuition** say about this situation? What would a wise person say about this situation? What does the wisest part of me want to tell me about this situation?

_____

_____

_____

_____

The answer to my question from my intuition:

_____

_____

_____

If you found this exercise a helpful way of working through situations you experience, visit http://www.newharbinger.com/52076 to download a worksheet version of it.

Going Deeper into Thoughts and Emotions

My first experience in therapy was with CBT. Despite my reluctance and resistance, my therapist required that I complete weekly diary cards on which I recorded my stressful thoughts and feelings, particularly about my body, and their antecedents: what specifically triggered stressful thoughts and feelings. Each week we would painstakingly go through each of my thoughts— when did I first think this thought? Where did it come from? What made me think it now?—and then we'd slowly dissect my thoughts from my feelings, which were more often than not, fused and confused. For instance, I'd confuse the thought *I feel gross today* (which is indeed a thought; "gross" is not a feeling) with the emotions underneath: sadness, loneliness, and anger. I'd confuse beliefs about my body with actual emotions, and thoughts about my body with facts. More often than not, when I was stressed about my body, it was because something outside of me was disturbing me—worry about the world, family, or my future—and this worry got displaced onto my body.

What this therapy did for me felt revolutionary. I could notice my thoughts rather than react to them as truth, and I could separate out my feelings from what I was thinking. Later on, I learned how to feel my emotions more accurately and to treat them as wise guides that I could rely on rather than suppress with patterns of anxiety.

Gaining such skills is a goal of psychotherapy. They are skills you can learn independently (although you might also consider therapy if you feel it will be beneficial and you have the means). In the following section we'll focus on discerning emotions, thoughts, and anxiety patterns that get displaced onto the body instead of on the actual problem.

The Boiling Pot of Anxiety

Imagine a large pot of water boiling vigorously on the stove. It has a lid, and the water is boiling so much that the lid is banging around and making a lot of noise. You can remove the lid, but the water inside is still boiling. This image describes what happens to us internally when we are caught in body hatred or anxiety. The boiling water is our true emotion, it is what is fueling all the noise, but the lid is what gets our attention and is where we tend to place our attention. What is on the surface, the banging lid, is all our thoughts of body hatred and feelings of anxiety, which are loud and uncomfortable. We can learn coping skills to help calm these down to some extent, but ultimately, the lid isn't the problem. The boiling water is where we need to place our attention. Body hatred thoughts and the anxiety they create are not true emotions; they are reactions to emotions, often serving to protect us from deeper, sometimes complex feelings. These reactions are called *defense mechanisms*. We do need to understand what we are feeling, but we also need to recognize that we developed these ways of protecting ourselves from feeling deeper emotions for very good reasons.

Defense mechanisms also include projection, repression, denial, rationalization, and displacement. But often, coping with anxiety is seen as the holy grail of self-help work. The assumption is that if only we could manage our anxiety, we would feel better. *If only I could cope with the thoughts of body anxiety that plague my days, I could get on with my life.* But while coping is a necessary set of skills, we can also over-cope—we can cope so well that the deeper reasons *why* we are anxious and hating our bodies do not get airtime. Identifying these deeper reasons is, to me, is the real, spiritual work of recovering from body hatred.

That said, working with anxiety is often the first step of the process. Anxiety can interfere with the ability to understand how thoughts of body hatred (the banging lids) are fueled by emotions, needs, and desires we're less conscious of (the boiling water). If our anxiety is low enough and tolerable, we can often identify the emotion underneath with relative ease. If our anxiety is too high, we can't do that. We need to lower anxiety first with anxiety management skills, which include:

1. **Problem solving:** If there is a problem you can solve that will decrease your anxiety, solve the problem rather than avoiding it.

2. **Observing and naming anxiety:** Paradoxically, taking a pause to consciously recognize that you feel anxious often begins reducing its intensity.

3. **Breathing:** Take one intentional breath. Pause. Take another. Repeat until the intensity of the anxiety decreases.

4. **Self-soothing:** Do something that calms you. Use calming words, smells, or relaxing activities. One thing is enough. What helps you feel safe and calm when you're anxious? You might take a moment to write some ideas down here.

_____

_____

Once your anxiety is lowered, often the true emotion can be more accurately felt and named.

The Magical Question

If you struggle with anxiety and body hatred, I don't have to tell you that it can be a tall order to get straight to an emotion when we are caught in our protective defense mechanisms. There's a reason we cover what we feel with anxiety or body hatred—sometimes what's boiling in the pot is incredibly inconvenient. The "magical question" helps to break the cycle of defense to get to what is underneath, the emotion or need in the boiling pot.

The magical question is a version of this:

If I weren't thinking about _____, what would I be thinking about or feeling?

For example:

If I weren't thinking about hating my body, what would I be thinking about?

If I weren't worried about my to-do list, what would I be feeling?

If I weren't anxious about food, what would I be feeling?

By questioning our default thinking and anxiety patterns, our minds and imaginations can open to thinking about anything else. The magical question helps us shift from being on autopilot to curiosity.

I remember being asked in a therapy session: what would I be thinking about if I weren't thinking about food? For a split second my brain short-circuited. I had never considered that there was another way; that I had permission to break the cycle and think about something I actually cared about. At that stage of my life, my answers were, "How unhappy I am in my relationship. How stressed I am with school and what I've committed to. How I feel confused by my family history and dynamics." All that was bubbling under the cover of food and body preoccupation.

This question stuck with me, and I return to it when I notice I'm caught in anxiety loops or habitual thinking that I know goes nowhere. My response is usually something more emotionally challenging that I don't really want to feel, but it's also usually far more meaningful in how it relates to my values, community, and spiritual life.

EXERCISE:
Answering the Magical Question

Take a moment to consider what you habitually think about and what might be under the surface.

My common anxious thoughts:

1. _____

2. _____

3. _____

Apply the Magic Question to each of the thoughts you listed:

If I weren't thinking #1, I would be thinking about or feeling

_____

_____

_____.

If I weren't thinking #2, I would be thinking about or feeling

_____

_____

_____.

If I weren't thinking #3, I would be thinking about or feeling

_____

_____

_____.

Updating Habitual Thinking

Thoughts happen in our minds as though they were reporters describing our experience, while emotions are felt in the body. When we can put words to what we are feeling, often we feel a deep sense of relief and containment, even if the emotion we're feeling and describing is a painful or uncomfortable one. It might seem obvious to say that thoughts are different from emotions, but it's really common to confuse the two. Thinking *I feel sad* is distinct from the actual emotion of sadness. Sadness in its felt sense is often a sensation of heaviness in the chest or stomach, and it often comes with the feeling of wanting to cry. As a therapist, it's fairly easy for me to tell if someone is feeling what they say they are feeling or if they are reporting what they *think* is happening, or what they think I want to hear, instead of what is really bubbling inside.

Thinking that is habitual and automatic can masquerade as truth or logic simply due to its familiarity and the influence of our cultures. We tend to confuse long-held thoughts with absolute truth, mistaking frequency and ingrained nature with validity. For example, it might take a tremendous leap of faith to question the belief that if you could just change how you look, you would finally feel better and be at peace. Or, if you've never taken a risk in your career, it can be hard to really believe that time off could be exactly what you need for the next stage of development personally and professionally. But often, when such patterns of thinking that we've been stuck in are brought to consciousness, they begin to lose their power over our lives.

EXERCISE:
Working with a Stressful Thought

This next journaling exercise is to help you track the origin of a thought so you can understand it more deeply, rather than reacting out of habit. To begin, identify a thought that causes you stress about your body. Reflect on the first time in your day that you noticed having a particular thought. For example, if you notice that you're having body worry thoughts like, *I don't like my body, I should start exercising more*, scan through your day and notice when this started. You might remember that a conversation with a family member made you uncomfortable and you started thinking about your body instead of feeling your discomfort with the conversation. Or maybe you notice that you looked at your email and something increased your anxiety. For just a moment, entertain the idea that perhaps your body stress was activated in the course of your day and is not an ever-present given.

Stressful body thought: _____

What tends to trigger this thought? Does it happen at a certain time of day, with particular people, or when you're doing something specific?

_____

_____

_____

Recall the most recent occurrence of this thought. Where were you, what were you doing, who were you with?

_____

_____

_____

_____

Explore the origins of this thought. When was the first time you had this thought in your life? What was happening then?

_____

_____

_____

Consider if there are others you know who also think this thought. Who do you know who also experiences this thought? Does this thought sound like the voice of someone you know, whether close to you or not?

_____

_____

Imagine if this thought served a purpose. What would that purpose be? You can ask wise mind to gain clarity on this.

_____

_____

Now, envision a scenario where you are no longer capable of thinking this thought. How would you feel? What would be at risk? What new possibilities would open up in your life?

_____

_____

_____

_____

If you find this approach to stressful thoughts helpful, you can visit http://www.newharbinger. com/52076 to download a worksheet version of this exercise.

Emotions as Guides

Body hatred can cause you to feel disconnected from true emotion, yet very connected to a near-constant state of stress. Separating emotions that are jumbled with history, anxiety, and thinking patterns can feel like the impossible task Psyche has on her hands as she first sees the pile of seeds in front of her. On a recovery path, it's important to start to feel and identify the more subtle layers of emotion underlying stress in order to more effectively get our physical, emotional, and spiritual needs met. Emotions tell us what we need, but tolerating and feeling emotions can be challenging. (You'll learn more calming skills in the following chapter.) For now, let's explore some reasons for why you might struggle with recognizing underlying emotions amidst body stress:

- **Overwhelming sensations:** Anxiety related to body stress carries intense physical sensations, including tightness in the chest, difficulty taking a deep breath, even physical numbness. These sensations can become so intense that they take your attention away from recognizing and understanding your underlying emotions.

- **Distorted thinking:** Body stress changes your thoughts and perceptions, leading to heightened self-doubt and exaggerated interpretations of situations. These thoughts make it challenging for you to accurately identify and label emotions.

- **Heightened focus on threats:** When anxiety and body stress take hold, your attention becomes fixated on potential threats or dangers —literally creating tunnel vision on possible danger, which is often your own body. This hyper-focus limits your ability to pay attention to and process more subtle emotions.

- **Fear of emotions:** Past experiences or societal influences may have caused you to develop an aversion towards certain emotions. For example, some families may be comfortable expressing sadness but have difficulty acknowledging anger, or vice versa. For people who have experienced periods of depression, emotions related to depression can feel really frightening. As a result, you may unknowingly avoid feeling and acknowledging certain emotions and express anxiety instead.

- **Limited emotional awareness or vocabulary:** You might not have been taught about emotions—their names, physical sensations, and what to do with them— because they were avoided in your family or culture. Perhaps emotions were seen as secondary to rational thinking. Or perhaps your temperament means emotions are not your primary language. Lack of emotional validation and mirroring can also interfere in knowing what you feel and what to do about it.

Which of these points resonate for you in relation to your emotional life? How have overwhelming sensations, distorted thinking, heightened focus on threats, fear of emotions, or limited emotional awareness impacted your emotional journey?

_____

_____

_____

_____

_____

_____

Validation and mirroring refer to the experience of having our emotions acknowledged and accepted as valid and understandable. Validation can look something like this: A child is visibly nervous and tense. An adult says, "You look nervous, do you want a hug?" It's clear the adult has recognized what the child is feeling and is willing to acknowledge it, in a way that helps the child in turn understand what they might be feeling and experience being soothed. Alternatively, a child sees an adult crying and witnesses others supporting the adult with a hug, care, or tending. If we are not validated or witness it happening for others, then we can have trouble knowing what we are feeling, leading to emotional confusion.

If you were raised in a family or culture that held beliefs about which emotions are acceptable—as we all were—you might have internalized these messages without knowing it. For example, Sam was raised in a family and culture in which anger was not okay. Anger was considered dangerous at worst and in bad taste at best. During her recovery, Sam learned that when she felt anxious about her body, it was often triggered by a true feeling of anger first. Learning to notice anger and unwind her inherited beliefs about anger being "bad" helped Sam set boundaries and make requests, leading to a sense of inner clarity and agency.

Are there certain emotions you notice are avoided, suppressed, or minimized in your family or culture? If so, what impact has this had on your experience of these emotions?

_____

_____

_____

_____

_____

_____

Learning the function of emotions so they become guides rather than burdens can help you gain inner clarity and increase self-trust. It can help unwind the internalized messages that emotions are not to be trusted when, in fact, emotions are deeply connected to intuition and signal that we are picking up on information our rational minds might be ignoring. Emotions have specific functions and knowing what our emotions are trying to tell us helps us connect to ourselves. With all emotions, there are natural, instinctual responses that arise when we feel them that prompt us to take specific actions. These are *action urges*. They help us respond to situations to ensure our well-being. We can learn to listen to these action urges and then to decide whether to act on them or not.

Here are a few examples of emotions and their functions:

- **Fear:** Indicates we are unsafe and have a need for safety.

- **Anger:** Signals a boundary has been crossed or a need is unmet.

- **Sadness:** Tells us something important needs to be grieved. We lost or don't have something we value.

- **Joy:** Signals that we are in need of celebration, expansion, and savoring goodness.

Note: Beware of body-based words masquerading as emotions. "Fat," for instance, is not a feeling. These words are masking an emotion we don't know how to name.

Pick a word or phrase you are in the habit of using about your body. It might be something you habitually worry about or judge about your body. What emotion comes up for you connected to this word? If you couldn't use body-based words to describe what you're feeling in this moment, what words would you use?

_____

_____

_____

_____

_____

_____

Often when people start down the path of reclaiming their body and getting to know their inner world, their emotional vocabulary is quite limited. "I'm fine" or "I feel weird" or "I'm good/bad" are common sentiments. This isn't due to a lack of intelligence or wisdom, as we've discussed. So often we learn to disconnect from feeling by staying mentally and physically busy. When we are busy—thinking about and managing our bodies, food, work, other people—it's harder to be in touch with our own emotions.

"Fat," "flabby," "gross," and "disgusting" are not emotions, yet are often used synonymously with "angry," "sad," "disappointed," or "lonely." Ultimately, when these words come up in our thoughts and reflections, it behooves us to protect our bodies by sparing them from harsh words and, instead, trying to name the deeper emotion we are feeling.

EXERCISE:
What Are You Feeling?

This practice is to help you identify what you are feeling and why so you can gather the wisdom of your emotions.

Directions: Find a private space to be alone for five minutes. Begin by taking five deep breaths, inviting yourself to settle into the present moment. Gently bring your attention to your body and complete this emotion check-in:

- What am I feeling emotionally? Circle which emotions resonate with you right now. There are no wrong emotions, but there may be emotions that feel more or less comfortable than others.

  - Joyful: excited, loved, warm, satisfied, amused

  - Fearful: worried, alarmed, helpless, uncomfortable, scared

  - Sad: lonely, heartbroken, gloomy, disappointed, grief

  - Shame: embarrassed, guilty, exposed, unaccepted, rejected

  - Angry: impatient, furious, enraged, irritated, resentful

  - Other: _____

- Once you have a sense of a specific emotion, ask this emotion directly: what do you want me to know?

_____

_____

_____

_____

_____

_____

- What does this emotion want to do, what is its impulse? (You might or might not act on this, but it's important to know the action urge that accompanies the emotion.)

_____

_____

_____

_____

_____

- Ask yourself "What do I need to do in this moment?" Here are some suggestions. Circle what speaks to you:

  - Connection needs

    · Hug someone.

    · Look through pictures.

    · Remember a funny memory.

    · Text a friend.

    · Make plans with someone.

    · Other: _____

  - Nature needs

    · Put your bare feet on the ground.

    · Dip your hands in a body of water or running water in the sink.

    · Water a plant.

    · Look at the sky.

    · Other: _____

- Nourishment needs

  - Cook or order a meal.

  - Eat a snack mindfully (without technology as a distraction).

  - Name five things you're grateful for.

  - Gently touch a part of your body that needs comfort and take three breaths.

  - Other: _____

- Spirituality needs

  - Meditate for five minutes.

  - Check in with your body and emotions.

  - Light a candle and be still for a moment.

  - Engage in a meaningful activity.

  - Go outside and notice something growing.

  - Other: _____

- Movement needs

  - Go for a walk.

  - Put on a song that always gets you dancing.

  - Set a timer for three minutes and shake every body part until it goes off.

  - Swim.

  - Other: _____

- Relationship needs

  - Hold a conversation with someone.

  - Set a boundary of some kind.

  - End a relationship.

- · Connect more deeply by sharing how you feel.

- · Other: _____

- Other needs (for example, financial, work, activism, sexual, medical, and communal) not on this chart:

_____

_____

Imagine what it might feel like to have this need met. Experiment with planning to meet this need, if possible. If your need feels too big for the present moment (for example, confronting a family member about an ongoing problem), go down a notch and see if there is a way you can find some ease and relief—or try breaking this large need down into smaller steps that you can more easily act on. (Perhaps you might choose not to attend the next family gathering or meet this person until you are ready to talk.)

_____

_____

_____

_____

_____

_____

_____

_____

If you find this exercise a useful one and want to do it again in the future, you'll find a worksheet for it at http://www.newharbinger.com/52076.

When Body Stress Transforms

As a therapist who works daily with clients who have body hatred and food stress, and as someone who has been through my own recovery process, I know not to trust my body judgment thoughts. It's not that I am immune to them; I simply don't trust them. What is so relieving about this is that when I do notice worry about my body, I immediately know there is something else going on that is more emotionally complex. It's as though I have a red flag system that tells me, "Something is happening here, pay attention." For example, on a recent vacation I noticed heightened body-conscious thoughts and judgments. Rather than sinking into body anxiety, I chose to be curious, asking my deeper instincts and intuition, which I imagine to be the mythological ants of the Psyche story, what was going on for me. I noticed that I felt uncomfortable about where we were staying, I didn't quite belong, and I felt sad about what it means to gentrify a beautiful wild place into a vacation town. These feelings and thoughts were layered on top of relational dynamics that made it hard for me to talk about what I was experiencing to the people I was with. Clarifying how I actually felt and what I was thinking helped open my body worry into a pathway of deep, inner connection to myself and my values. The pile of body worry and physical anxiety had masked my true emotions of grief, gratitude, and acknowledgement of the complex privileges at play on our trip. My ability to be curious transformed body worry into something not necessarily fixable, but more real and honest.

This is what I hope to be possible for you with regular practice of these skills, trusting that there is a paradox in which hating your body can be a pathway to soul. Identifying thoughts, working with the three states of mind, and naming emotions and needs are humble, grounded psychological skills that organize our inner worlds so we can make room for ourselves and our heart callings.

CHAPTER 4

Listening to Your Body and Deep Self

The focus of this chapter is the shift from thinking about your body to feeling your body; from assessing and critiquing your physical self to inhabiting and sensing it. In the last chapter we focused on sorting and organizing your thoughts and emotions. This chapter is about deepening into your body through felt, somatic experience. Clarissa Pinkola Estés (1992, 212) described this shift from assessing to feeling that is vital to body hatred recovery as follows:

> There is no "supposed to be" in bodies. The question is not size or shape or years of age, or even having two of everything, for some do not. But the wild issue is, does this body feel, does it have right connection to pleasure, to heart, to soul, to the wild? Does it have happiness, joy? Can it in its own way move, dance, jiggle, sway, thrust? Nothing else matters.

The path from body hatred to body peace requires that we learn to feel our bodies and our feelings, to recover our connection to our instincts, our wildness, our intuition. To do this, we need to do three things.

One is to break the habit of *not feeling*. This means we have to consciously practice feeling our bodies. Many of us are habituated to simply not feeling much in our bodies. We practice feeling to feel more. Movement, meditation, and somatically informed therapy are great ways to slow down enough to actually feel our bodies. This chapter will offer tools to explore these methods on your own.

Another thing we need to do is slow down. Busyness, distraction, and overstimulation are not conducive to feeling. In fact, they do the opposite—they hijack our attention and help us do anything but feel ourselves. We have to slow down and eliminate distractions to feel more. There's really no way around it. Slowing down with awareness is an inescapable need if we are to inhabit our bodies more fully.

The third thing we need to do to recover our connection to ourselves to increase our tolerance for "being with"—from distress to pleasure. A primary reason we dissociate from our bodies is due to the challenge of feeling distress, intense emotions, or longing. Developing a capacity to "be with" without judgment is a key to body freedom, because once we can be with ourselves, we can trust our ability to tolerate what we are experiencing with awareness rather than resistance or critique.

Descent of Inanna

The ancient Sumerian myth of Inanna is a guide for this journey into our bodies, out of body hatred into communion with ourselves. This myth echoes the primal need to be with our pain, our feelings, and ourselves—something that can be so hard to do when hatred and shame about the body has become our norm—as a way to come back to life. There are many translations and interpretations of the Inanna myth; the following overview of her story is based on the translation from Wolkstein and Kramer (1983):

> Inanna is the Queen of Heaven and Earth. Her sister is Ereshkigal, the Queen of the Underworld. One day, Inanna is called to the underworld to pay respects to her sister following the death of Ereshkigal's husband. Inanna knows the risk of entering the underworld and prepares by asking her aide Ninshubur to keep watch. If she doesn't return within three days, Ninshubur should seek help from the other gods.
>
> Inanna enters the underworld with all her upper-world regalia—clothing, jewelry, stones, and more. The gatekeepers of the underworld announce to Ereshkigal that Inanna has come, and Ereshkigal insists that Inanna enter as everyone enters the underworld—naked and surrendered. At each of the seven gates Inanna encounters, she is stripped of one layer of her upper-world vestments. At the bottom of the descent, Inanna encounters her sister and Ereshkigal kills her. Inanna is hung on a meathook and her flesh rots.
>
> Meanwhile, following Inanna's orders, Ninshubur appeals to the gods, but only one of them will help save Inanna. Enki, god of water and wisdom, agrees to help, and with the dust from under his fingernail, he creates two tiny beings—the galtur and the kurgarra, the "little mourners"—to mourn with Ereshkigal. Enki gives the galtur the Water of Life, and he gives

the kurgarra the Food of Life; these items will restore Inanna. The little mourners are such small beings that they're able to move through the gates of the underworld undetected.

When these dust-beings reach Ereshkigal, she's wailing, as though she's in labor. In fact, different translations describe the wailing as labor pains. As she wails, these two dust-beings wail with Ereshkigal.

She says, "Oh, oh! My insides!"

They say, "Oh, oh, oh! Your insides!"

"Oh, oh, oh! My pain!"

They echo, "Oh, oh, oh! Your pain!"

As they echo, they soothe Ereshkigal so much that she asks the little mourners what they would like in return for their service. They ask for the flesh of Inanna, which Ereshkigal gives them. They sprinkle the Water and Food of Life over her body, and Inanna is restored to life. Then, she is able to pass with them back through the seven gates to the upper world.

Inanna has been changed as a result of this journey. When someone eats something in the underworld, they then belong to the underworld, and Inanna ate the Water and Food of Life. Now, she is not simply a princess coming back to her throne—she has been initiated into the ways of the underworld. So, a sacrifice is required. To pay her dues, Inanna has to send a substitute to live in the underworld in her place. She sends her husband, Dumuzi, who did not honor her while she was gone, and she also sends his sister, Geshtinanna, who ends up sharing the year with him.

This myth can serve as a template for recovering ourselves, for making contact with our own depths after living with the stifling, hollow reality of body hatred. Making contact with our bodies can feel like a descent journey— a descent from the mind, critique, and reason into our bodies, sensations, and instincts. Then, once we are there, we need the sacred echo that the galtur and kurgarra, the "little mourners," provide Ereshkigal in all her wailing. We need to be echoed, with care, not simply reassured; for our emotions to be recognized, not simply coped with. Being with ourselves in pain, pleasure, feeling, and need opens us to new life, a way of relating with ourselves that creates something new and altogether different.

Whether we know it consciously or not, most of us are familiar with this pattern of descent and rebirth. The way this pattern might appear in your life is when you feel a call towards change, possibly first through noticing dissatisfaction with your life as it is and a longing for something unnamable. The call for change might eventually reveal a longing for something new and exciting, like travel, a family, or a career change. But if the call is asking for deep transformation, it often puts you into the land of symbolic death and rebirth, even if it sounds beautiful. The call to recover from body hatred can be transformational, and this myth offers solace that something new will emerge from the journey.

Breaking the Habit of Numbing

Once you become tired of fighting your body, you can start to learn how to sense your body from the inside out, rather than maintaining a distanced, critical eye on yourself. We can imagine this process through the lens of the myth of Inanna. Just as she sheds her upper world regalia to enter the underworld to mourn with her sister, we learn to shed the layers of upperworld acculturation—the ideas we get from culture, family, and society—so we can arrive in the underworld of our particular feelings and sensations. The upperworld regalia we surrender include inherited thoughts, ideas, and "should" about our bodies; what we discover in the underworld are the less familiar lands of our bodies and feelings.

This might sound frightening, but remember that from a depth psychological perspective, the underworld is the unconscious—the parts of ourselves that are unfamiliar, that have been under-felt and under-recognized, and that are longing to come to consciousness. It is these parts of us that give us guidance for our life purpose, griefs, and joys. In other words, this is the place of soul. Through the lens of DBT, this inner soulfulness is wise mind, and the ability to contact and feel your body, just as it is, can be a central pathway into this intuitive center.

Ultimately, whether you take a behavioral or depth psychological approach to what's happening, when you start to listen to your body, you'll find that it has its own voice, one that is separate from your normal train of thoughts about your body. This deeper listening begins to yoke you back to yourself, which many find deeply relieving after enduring the separation from the body and inner self that body hatred causes. As Fuller (2017, 97) states, "Dieting never allowed me to even know what I liked because a diet does not trust the eater to know such things." In other words, there is distance between self-awareness and your body after enduring body hatred (and dieting). Body awareness and feeling help shift that pattern of distance so you can discern what you want and need, both as a body and as a soul.

Bodies speak with their own particular languages—their own particular combinations of sensation, sound, inner images, and intuition, depending on our temperament. The following practice can help you begin to listen to how your body speaks to you. The combination of sensing (right brain) and naming what you are feeling (left brain) decreases emotional confusion and dysregulation, offering a powerful healing effect by bridging the two hemispheres of the brain and increasing your sense of self-trust and regulation.

To begin cultivating this skill, set aside at least five minutes, find a private space, and eliminate distractions like technology, food, or noise as much as possible. The goal of the meditative activity you're about to do is to notice what you are feeling and experiencing without judgment. You'll want to identify and name what you're feeling, but avoid making stories about what you feel, including making meaning of what you notice or trying to figure out why you feel what you feel. Here, we're trying to feel somatically and not to think or reason cognitively, which can contribute to feeling far away from ourselves.

EXERCISE:
Feeling Your Body from the Inside Out

Complete the following questionnaire as you listen to your body. Notice how you sense your body on the spectrum of the following physical sensations, marking the degree to which you feel each sensation. For example, for the Hot–Cold scale, you would mark an X in the middle if you are at a comfortable temperature, neither hot nor cold:

Hot _____ Cold

Tingling _____ Numb

Buzzy _____ Still

Tense _____ Relaxed

Hungry _____ Full

Satisfied _____ Unsatisfied

Other sensations you notice: _____

_____

_____

Then, consider...

- **Sensation:** Where in your body do you feel the most sensation? Head, shoulders, chest, stomach, back, legs, feet? Somewhere else?

    _____

    _____

- **Intensity:** How intense are your body sensations right now on a 1–10 scale?

    _____

- **Familiarity:** Is this a familiar or unfamiliar feeling?

    _____

- **Tolerance:** Is this feeling tolerable or intolerable?

    _____

- If the intensity is too high or it is too uncomfortable, pull back and try to approach the feeling slowly, imagining feeling only one drop of the feeling at a time.

Move (Differently) to Feel More

If you are recovering from body hatred, then your relationship with movement is probably complicated. Often the idea of movement is bound up with attempts to change or control our bodies. What has "movement" meant to you up to this point? Was there a point when movement—moving your body to get around, explore, or have fun—shifted to "exercise"? When labels like "exercise" come up, how do you feel? Conversely, have there been moments or times when you've experienced movement that has felt good and nourishing?

_____

_____

_____

_____

_____

A history of overexercising or shame about moving your body can stop you from learning to listen to your body through movement. Yet bodies want to move. You can support yourself in learning to sense your body by moving in ways that feel good and nourishing, rather than dissociative or painful.

Sarah experienced a profound shift in how she felt about her body when she learned how to move in ways that felt pleasurable rather than out of obligation. She explained how dancing, in particular, felt really good and helped her want to "be in" her body more. "There was more than just, 'I'm gonna go to yoga class 'cause I need to exercise.' It was like, 'I'm gonna do this because this feels so good.'" Dancing encouraged her to follow intuitive, pleasurable, and nourishing sensations, supporting her ability to be in her body rather than dissociating through thinking about her body.

We are talking about movement that is guided by the body itself. It can be dancing, walking, running, yoga—the point is that the body is felt and listened to as the guide, not the instructor or exercise plan. Using the body as guide serves two purposes:

1. Shifting from thinking to feeling: Movement that is guided by the body rather than the mind is a way to soften your mind, allowing emotions and thoughts to emerge that are usually kept under the surface of your awareness.

2. Experiencing increased sensation: Movement facilitates increased proprioceptive awareness, which is the ability to sense your body. This might be a new skill for you, since body sensations tend to be desensitized after years of enduring body hatred.

Take a second to think about some forms of movement that you think will feel good to you. If you have trouble with this, ask your body directly, as best you can, to come up with an idea to try. What does your body tell you it needs?

_____

_____

Is there an opportunity for you to practice this activity at some point over the next week or so? Give it a try—and then come back to this workbook to journal about the experience. What was it like? What challenges came up? Did you enjoy it?

_____

_____

_____

_____

_____

Move to Connect to Your True Hunger

As you begin to sense your body, a new relationship with your body can emerge in which wildness and instinct are accessed, previously unknown parts of yourself begin to show up, and emotions, needs, and desires become clearer. Your true hunger is coming into consciousness—the guiding inner hunger that pulls you towards what means something to you on a soul level. Somatically focused Jungian analyst Marion Woodman (1985, 60) described the centrality of the body in developing a stable and secure sense of self: "The body has a wisdom of its own. However slowly and circuitously that wisdom manifests, once it is experienced it is a foundation, a basis of knowing that gives confidence and total support to the ego." This is what it means to live "in your body"—your body becomes an ally on your life path, rather than a project to complete or a burden to endure. Your body holds your instincts, hunger, and knowing. Movement helps anchor these aspects somatically and shift you out of just thinking about what you want and feel.

After I had begun writing and teaching a course on the idea of true hunger as a guiding force, I was at the weekly dance class that I attend as my form of spiritual practice and fellowship. I was in a PhD program, had a full psychotherapy practice, and had recently finished writing a book about DBT. I was steeped in work and learning, and my life seemed full to the brim with purpose and meaning. As I was dancing, I was listening to my body and breath when, like a bolt of lightning, I felt and heard, "I want to take a break and have a baby." Uh oh. This was inconvenient; my mind could not have been more surprised—and yet my body was so at ease. It was as though the longing my body had been holding finally got airtime; my body relaxed even while my mind scrambled to organize around this epiphany.

Cognitively, I had deep ambivalence around becoming a mother. I felt confused about the impact of a child on my own life and the planet. Yet I allowed this breakthrough of consciousness to nourish me; I stayed curious about what I was feeling. And I found that I did, in fact, long to reorient my energies to more domestic and familial ones. I did long for the initiation of becoming a mother. I wanted to have a baby. There were questions and uncertainties. I felt unready for a baby, but there was a deep pull toward this change that I couldn't ignore. This is an example of true hunger breaking through consciousness— a deeper guiding instinct that I previously had only had access to through my dreams came through a somatic experience. In 2019 I gave birth to my daughter.

Movement helps us feel like we are actually here, that we are flesh and blood and part of the world around us. It helps us connect with nature instead of being dissociated into patterns of self-attack and self-control. Movement is a practice just as sitting still to meditate is a practice. Movement helps us connect to what our bodies *want* to do, rather than what we are demanding they do, and this, in turn, helps us listen to soul-level longing. Movement that is guided by pleasure and intuition helps yoke us to our instincts, our deep knowing, and our purpose in the world.

EXERCISE:
Song Shuffle

I learned this three- to five-minute practice (the length of one song) from Rochelle Sheick, founder of Qoya Inspired Movement. Begin by choosing a playlist on any media player you use. Find a private space with enough room to move. Put the playlist on shuffle and press play. Don't move until your body wants to move. Your guiding question is, "If my body could lead, how would it move to this song?" There is no right or wrong way to move your body, beyond being mindful of any injuries or physical limitations. Movements could be big and expansive or small and subtle. Your body might want to lie on the floor and take a breath. Try to soften any judgment or criticism towards yourself, your body, or movement. Notice what it feels like to simply let your body lead, with curiosity rather than critique. Then, process your experience.

1. What did you notice in your body when the song came on? What was your first impulse?

    _____

    _____

2. How would you describe your movements? What felt good to your body? What did your body say "no" to?

    _____

    _____

3. What was it like to let your body guide your movement? Was this familiar or unfamiliar to you?

    _____

    _____

4. What surprised you about this practice?

    _____

    _____

Slow Down to Feel More

Imagine this: You're at a crowded party, surrounded by people and sounds and food, every-thing around you trying to get your attention. Someone you know comes up to you and sincerely asks how you are. At that moment, someone bumps into you while reaching for a drink. Then you suddenly pick up a tidbit of another conversation that catches your ear. If you haven't already had a panic attack by simply reading this, great. In this scenario, it might be a relief to know someone wants to make real, emotional contact with you, but it would be hard to engage authen-tically with so many external distractions pulling you outside of yourself (not to mention the internal ones getting activated by being in a social setting like this).

Often when we are asked to feel our bodies and emotions there are so many distractions, so many voices to drown out. It takes intentionally slowing down and eliminating distractions to begin to feel more. This can be a luxury for most of us who lead full lives with technology and kids and work and stress. But it's part of the process to shift from body hatred to body respect—the busyness-overstimulation train has to take a rest so you can slow down enough to feel more.

We can imagine slowing down, with care, by thinking about how Inanna is called to pay her respects to Ereshkigal. It is inconvenient and does not necessarily fit in the flow of our daily lives to be that intentional with ourselves. Yet recovery from body hatred is sacred work. Understanding that it requires us to be inconvenienced is important—it is inconvenient, and essential, to break the habit of going too quickly in order to make space for ourselves and for the subtle feelings, dreams, and needs that might be overlooked in the normal pace of life. The following three exer-cises are designed to support you in slowing down to feel more.

EXERCISE:
Slow Down Your Breath

This is a simple practice. Right now, slow down your breath…. Then slow it down just a tiny bit more.

Notice what happens in your body when you slow down your breath. What happens in your mind?

Do this in moments when you don't think you can slow down, but know you need to. You might try breathing slowly during the morning hustle, while in a conversation, on a grocery store run, or during the midday grind. See what happens.

EXERCISE:
One Drop at a Time

When we slow down, an inevitable challenge arises: "What do I do with what I feel? What if what I feel when I slow down is too much, overwhelming, or out of control?" This is why we go slow. The "one drop" practice is a way to slow down, gently and with some control, so you don't feel flooded with feelings that you don't know what to do with. In somatic psychology this is called "titration." We slow down until we feel, and then we titrate by feeling "one drop" of the feeling at a time, backing off if we need to, so we can acclimate to what we're feeling rather than being overwhelmed by it. Learning how to feel your internal world safely can give you the courage to feel more and more.

Let's try titration now.

1.   Set a five-minute timer.

2.   Take a breath to land in your body and the present moment. Get present by noting the date, time, and your current location.

3.   Shifting inwards, notice what you feel: do you feel body sensations? Emotions? Urges?

4.   Where in your body do you feel a sensation most clearly?

5.   Put a word to one sensation you notice in your body.

6.   Imagine only feeling one drop (or a half a drop) of this sensation you feel.

7.   Back off of what you're feeling: shift your attention to the outside, look around your space for a couple moments to decrease the sensation.

8.   Imagine returning to your feelings—just one drop only.

9.   If it feels tolerable, add one more drop of feeling.

10.   Shift your attention to the outside world again.

Continue this practice, adding one drop at a time or staying with one drop for the whole five minutes. If "one drop" isn't working, you can try another metaphor: imagine having a volume dial and turning the volume "up" or "down" to see where it feels good to land in your body.

When you're done, reflect on the experience. Was it helpful to you to practice this way? Or was it challenging? Either way, you might consider making this a regular daily practice to continue building this skill and your ability to use it in the moment. If you are noticing very intense sensations, you might work with a therapist or body worker to support your body's ability to titrate and shift between states and feelings.

EXERCISE:
Create Your Own Ritual to Slow Down

The core of DBT is mindfulness. We practice paying attention to the present moment on purpose so we can shift from reactivity to noticing, from emotional dysregulation to curiosity, from dissociation to presence. One of the hardest things for students and therapists of DBT to do is establish a mindfulness practice, even for just a few minutes a day. What can help is shifting from thinking of a mindfulness practice as a *practice* to thinking of it as a *ritual* that has meaning and purpose on a soul level. This exercise can help you create an intentional time and space to slow down, in a ritualized way, and be consistent in connecting with yourself. A ritual has these features:

1. **Repetition:** A ritual is practiced at the same time of day or year, in the same interval (for example: daily, weekly, quarterly).

2. **Structure:** A ritual has a beginning, middle and an end.

3. **Connection to the sacred:** A ritual has the focus of connecting us to something sacred. Usually rituals are done in community to create social cohesion around shared values, but individual rituals offer intimacy with what we personally hold to be sacred.

An example from my own life: I have a journaling ritual with a friend that we have done for years now. I prefer to wake up before my family does, when it's still quiet and dark. I make coffee and find a comfortable place to sit. I journal for about 10 minutes in a structured way and send my writing to my friend. If I have time, I will work with a dream I remember. We reply to one another later in the day with a brief message honoring whatever the other has sent. All in all, it's about a twelve-minute practice. This writing practice is intentionally inconvenient—it's a time I have to carve out, by always waking up before I want to—but it's sacred to me: it connects me to myself and my friend. Of course, some days I can't do my ritual; sometimes I only have a couple minutes and I do what I can. But it's less important to me that I do it every day without fail than it is that I *have* a ritual, one that is a continual thread in my life and connects me to myself and to others. It's not about perfection and discipline, it is a regular, ritualized practice and self-commitment, one that nourishes me.

Examples of ritual practices include dancing, meditating, journaling, walking in nature, stretching, bathing, or looking out your window. The following prompts can help you come up with a ritual of your own to slow down and connect to yourself. The prompts focus on only three steps, but you can use another sheet of paper for more steps if you need to.

My intention for the ritual: _____

When I will engage in my ritual: _____ (morning, evening; when you can be quiet is best)

How often I will engage in my ritual: _____ (daily, weekly, monthly, on important days)

What I will do in my ritual:

Example:

1. Light a candle.

2. Meditate for five minutes.

3. Blow out the candle.

Your ritual:

1. _____

2. _____

3. _____

Plan when you will engage in your ritual. After trying it once, return to this workbook and write about your feelings and reactions. What did you feel as you engaged in your ritual? How did you feel after? Does it need some tweaking in terms of timing or action steps?

_____

_____

_____

_____

Increasing Tolerance for "Being With" Yourself

The myth of Inanna tells us about the transformative power of being with someone in their pain without trying to change it. The "little mourners" offer a sacred echo and presence to Ereshkigal in the depths of her pain; they do not reassure or fix. These tiny beings are insignificant enough to pass through the gates of the underworld as particles of dirt. Yet how often is the tiny gesture the most impactful? A head tilt, the moment someone leans in to feel *with* us rather than creating distance—these can be enough to give us the feeling that someone is truly listening, without trying to change what we feel. In our own journeys, we are exploring how to be with ourselves in this same caring, nonjudgmental way, as a way to increase our ability to sit with ourselves and, gradually, shift from body hatred to inner peace.

I remember the moment I stopped some of my most persistent eating disorder behaviors on my recovery journey. I was reading a book about spirituality and food. The essence of what I was reading was, "If you are present with yourself, in the moment, with your feelings, you won't have to run away." This was not new information, but in this moment it was as though a switch flipped in me, my years of therapy clicked into place, and I could sense how by being present, feeling what I felt, I wouldn't have to run from a threat that was largely internal. In this moment of epiphany, I finally truly understood the notion of being with myself, with care, without running away, and what this might open up for me.

These moments of epiphany are real. Sometimes, after a long process of working on a project, our unconscious forces gather together and spark new understanding, clarity, and change. For me, this epiphanic breakthrough was foundational to the next stages of my recovery journey; it helped me have a felt, embodied understanding of how being with my emotions and sensations was essential for body peace.

When we begin to listen to our bodies and internal worlds, it's normal for strong emotions and discomfort to arise. (This is especially true if you have a trauma history, and in that case you might consider working with a trusted guide or therapist for additional support.) Yet the ability to be with ourselves, without changing or controlling what we feel, has the paradoxical effect of providing comfort and relief. For example, Lauren explained how she learned how to sit with her emotions when she feels out of control, rather than controlling her body as a reaction to distress: "When I feel out of control, I often want to control my body. However, I also value my well-being and peace of mind, so I try to remain in the moment and accept the lack of control and feel it all." For Lauren, learning to tolerate moments of feeling out of control was essential for body hatred to stop controlling her. When we learn to "be with" ourselves, we can shift from body hatred to embodied peace.

While self-soothing and comforting might be important skills for this journey, we have a foundational need for presence over reassurance, validation and tolerance for discomfort over soothing and comforting. The paradox is that when we are able to *be with* our inner experience, just as it is, whether it's good or bad, we tend to feel comforted, as we see in the myth of Inanna.

Lily described an experience with a therapist that was transformative for her. After her cancer diagnosis and treatment, Lily experienced tremendous anxiety and fear of cancer recurrence. She sought therapy to help her with this anxiety. She explained to her therapist that she was worried she had cancer again, expecting the therapist to reassure her that she probably didn't. Instead, her therapist simply echoed back, "Maybe you have cancer again." Lily felt flooded with relief that someone was able to be with her in her fear, with compassion, in the unknown. She found it was more soothing than any superficial reassurance she'd received, and it transformed her experience of anxiety. In that moment, she became larger than her fear; she could hold her fear and anxiety, rather than fight or resist it.

In the DBT class I co-teach, we often talk about the possibility of relying too much on certain skills. There *is* such a thing as over-coping: we can overuse distraction and self-soothing skills instead of developing the ability to problem solve or simply tolerate our troubles. So much of life is boring, distressing—and awe-inspiring. Being with these human experiences, all of them, connects us to life. Shifting from *coping* to *being with*, even our pain, can help us feel more alive and more human.

Imagine Inanna emerging from the underworld. She is not a glorious butterfly; she was murdered and brought back to life. The wisdom earned in this descent and rebirth process is not simply a shiny and clean revamp. Rather, it's maturity: the experience of being changed and becoming stronger, a more capacious person than we once were. The ability to tolerate deep, abiding feeling changes us. In therapy, much of our time is spent learning to cope and then unlearning how to cope. It's a spiral—we learn ways to soothe and distract to stop unhealthy behaviors, but at a certain point we have to face why those behaviors were happening in the first place, and that's where tolerating and *being with* is central. And this learning changes us. Being changed is the best we can hope for, and it happens through a true initiation process where our suffering and wounding results in real transformation, not a temporary boost in self-confidence.

Let's work on some skills to help you develop your ability to *be with*.

EXERCISE:
Hearing the Inner Echo

Notice the differences in how you feel as you read the following scenarios:

1. You get an upsetting phone call and now you have to rearrange your whole day, maybe even your week. You're irritable and frustrated. Then you run into a friend. You tell your friend what happened and they reply, "Well, look on the bright side, there's a reason for everything so it's going to work out."

2. You get an upsetting phone call that made you have to rearrange your whole day, perhaps even your week. You're irritable and frustrated when you run into a friend. You tell your friend what happened. Your friend pauses, as if thinking about what you said. They say, "Wow, that really sucks. I want to hear more."

What do you notice as you read these scenarios? Sometimes we might need a shift in perspective; sometimes some reassurance does feel like the right thing. But if we are more familiar with other people not picking up on or understanding our emotions, then what we need more is accurate, caring validation. We will explore this idea more in the following exercise.

EXERCISE:
What Does Emotional Validation Sound Like?

Imagine the last time you felt the following emotions. Consider what you needed to hear from someone when you were feeling each emotion. Notice if others tried to console or reassure, and imagine being validated or accurately witnessed instead. Notice what it feels like when you imagine hearing what you needed to hear in the midst of an emotion.

The last time I felt scared, I needed to hear _____.

The last time I felt angry, I needed to hear _____.

The last time I felt sad, I needed to hear _____.

The last time I felt lonely, I needed to hear _____.

The last time I felt excited, I needed to hear _____.

The last time I felt happy, I needed to hear _____.

Once you've completed the above, consider: how can you continue bringing this skill of witnessing and validating deep feeling instead of soothing, reassurance, or consolation—to your day-to-day life? How might this ability inform your relationship to yourself, your relationships with others, your relationship to struggle, and your ongoing journey to attune to your soul hunger instead of struggling with body hatred?

_____

_____

_____

_____

_____

_____

Over the next week or so, keep an eye out for situations that provoke strong feelings—about your body or anything else. See if you can maintain self-awareness and catch yourself in these moments. Then see if you can pause and witness and validate what you feel rather than acting on it immediately; see if you then choose wiser, more deliberate, kinder actions. Finally, come back to this workbook, and write about the experience.

_____

_____

_____

_____

_____

_____

_____

_____

_____

_____

_____

CHAPTER 5

Soul Recovery

On the journey to make peace with our bodies, we begin to notice all the ways normative diet culture interferes with this process. It's really hard to feel at peace with and in our bodies when we are embedded in a culture that consistently emphasizes how certain bodies or body parts are wrong and in need of fixing. In addition to the behavioral and somatic work we've done so far through this book—working with thoughts, identifying emotions, and increasing a felt sense of the body—body hatred recovery is also a process of soul recovery that helps us detach from the toxic aspects of a body-shaming culture and reclaim a sense of self that is purposeful and sacred.

During her recovery from body hatred, Priya learned that listening to her body led her to listening to deeper longings. She found that when she wasn't preoccupied with thinking about her body, she was thinking about the world and her place in it. She found her way to meaningful work that served her community and provided a sustainable living. That kind of change—listening to soul-level hunger and guidance—is the work you'll explore in this chapter.

Making Contact with Your Daimon and Anima Mundi

While the journey outlined in this book is focused on the experiences women have of their bodies, the ultimate journey you're taking is between you and yourself, your soul, particularly in its relationship to the world. There is little good to connecting to ourselves if we don't connect to the world's calling and need. Instead of embarking on yet another personal development project, the underlying need in body hatred recovery is to connect to what depth psychologists call the *anima mundi*—the world's soul, the spirit within the material world.

One way to begin to connect to the world's soul is to connect to your own. James Hillman (1996, 8), the founder of a branch of depth psychology called archetypal psychology, describes vocation as a calling from an inner *daimon*, or soul-companion: "This daimon remembers what is in your image and belongs to your pattern, and therefore your daimon is the carrier of your destiny." To Hillman, listening to one's daimon is a process of re-membering, contacting an aspect of soul that is not discovered so much as it is brought into consciousness. Again, the unconscious is what we experience when we dream at night, or where we go when we trail off in thought or daydreams, and it's where we experience the sacred. It's also where the blueprints for the acorn to grow into the oak tree, as we talked about in chapter 1, reside. As Woodman (1980, 100) puts it, women "must learn to hear the voice of their own abandoned Self and thus reconnect with their own inner mystery." So often this abandoned Self is the body itself—how it wants to move, eat, feel, and act—and listening to the body is listening to the call of this inner daimon, the voice of one's destiny.

So how do we do this? How do we make contact with our souls in a culture that has little regard for things like dreams, intuition, or the sacredness of the unconscious? The first step, as I see it, is to recognize the hunger for soul, the sacred hunger for *something more*. Allow this hunger to guide, inform, and lead you towards yourself. You protect this center by staying embodied and *taking your eyes back* from a culture that has hijacked who gets to do the seeing (I explain this concept a little later on in this chapter). Then you can engage in life in ways that honor your daimon, your calling. This can happen in many ways—community work, activism, homemaking, artmaking, journaling, ritual, ceremony, being in and with nature.

For me, dreamwork is a sacred practice that opens my ear to the underworld, like Inanna hearing the call from Ereshkigal—I listen to the unconscious with curiosity and reverence. Often dreamwork guides my work and waking life decision-making. Later in this chapter, I will lead you through dreamwork in case that is something that speaks to you.

The main skills you will learn in this chapter will help you to:

1. Identify where you are *stuffed* and *starved* in order to sense your soul hunger.

2. *Take your eyes back* to practice seeing clearly and staying in your body.

3. Connect with soul through nature and dreamwork to find personal meaning and guidance for your life.

Stuffed and Starved: Nourishment and Depletion

A guiding question to connect with soul is *What am I hungry for?* Recognizing what we are hungry for on a physical, emotional, and spiritual level often helps anchor us more deeply into ourselves, our calling, and our life purpose. Realizing where and in what ways we are hungry helps point us toward soul.

Often, in the fullness and busyness of consumer culture, we are stuffed with things that are half-satisfying, while starved of what might actually satisfy us. This dynamic of being stuffed and starved puts us on the merry-go-round of seeking out what we think will satisfy, often finding that we need more and more to fulfill a hunger that cannot actually be filled by outside sources. Woodman (1982, 13), understood this inner desire that often emerges in our quiet moments at night, at home, alone as a rebellion to a "wolfish" pursuit of perfection that is experienced during daylight: "The wolf attitude which demands more and more and more during the day, howls I want, I want, I want at night… The demon who wears the mask of respectability during the day shows his real face at night." This inner howling is the call of our true hunger asking to be fed.

Here are some examples of this stuffed-and-starved feeling as it can manifest in body hatred and many other life domains:

- **Body:** You work so hard to get your body to an idealized state of health, size, weight, or fitness, yet you keep finding that there is no finish line. You are inundated with suggestions for attaining perfected health and you feel deeply undernourished.

- **Career:** You have followed a hoped-for career path and you finally landed your dream job, gotten into college, or maybe are earning your dream income, yet you now experience a sense of being tricked since you don't really feel better.

- **Relationships:** You finally met the person you want to be with long-term and now you're realizing even that person won't be entirely enough to satisfy the longing you're desperately attempting to fill.

- **Productivity:** You are always trying to get on top of it all, yet no matter what you do—no matter how organized you get, whatever new system you employ—there's a sense that you will never actually be able to catch your breath; there'll always be another mountain to scale.

- **Possessions:** You have all the clothing and tech gadgets you could reasonably need or want, but still there is always something else you want to buy or attain while knowing deep down that it won't actually satisfy you long-term.

Do any of these resonate with you? If so, which ones?

_____

_____

What is an example of a situation in your own life in which you feel like you keep trying to attain a particular goal, but there is no arrival?

_____

_____

_____

_____

Your Body is a Project

In a stuffed-and-starved culture, women in particular are trained to treat the body as an ongoing life project. The term "Body Project" was coined by historian Joan Jacobs Brumberg in her 1998 book by that name. This cultural attitude teaches women that their body is something to be worked on, exercised, and dieted, rather than listened to. When we are caught in the Body Project attitude, we might feel that our bodies will betray us if we stop working on them. We might also feel confused about our larger purpose in the world, because the Body Project is a wildly effective distraction from deeper questions. For some women, the Body Project can look like an insatiable need to stay busy, to regulate the body in whatever way possible, and not question external authorities, including those that only seek to sell yet another solution to your perceived body problems.

In what ways does your body still feel like a project to complete? Do you sense this attitude has interfered or will interfere in other goals or desires you seek to pursue?

_____

_____

_____

Not Enough-ness

Another characteristic of being stuffed-and-starved is that no matter what you do or how amazing your accomplishments are, you tend to minimize your successes and press on. This attitude often results in a compulsive cycle of being unable to digest and celebrate your worth and work. You might have chronic feelings of not being enough, doing enough, or having enough. The mid-life (or quarter-life) crisis is a common trope, but it often happens when the soul has been ignored for too long, when you have been overworking in ways that were expected of you but are, in some fundamental way, unsatisfying.

Many people arrive at or complete a particular stage in life only to discover an underlying sense of restlessness and desperation. This often-unnamable longing for something more is the soul speaking up and saying, "Something needs to change. I'm hungry for more. I'm tired of not enough." In other words, in an attempt to compensate for feeling like *you* are not enough, you build a life that is simply *not enough* to the soul—and eventually, there is a reckoning.

In what ways have you experienced not-enoughness? Have you felt as though you, yourself, were not enough in some way? Have you experienced lack in your external life? In what ways?

_____

_____

_____

Family Patterns

Stuffed-and-starved dynamics can often be clearly seen in nuclear family structures. In some families, despite plenty of resources or access to resources, there is a sense that something crucial is missing. Some families are stuffed with activities, too-full houses, or too many responsibilities but starved of what is truly needed—such as real community, reliable support, time in nature, play, clear communication, loving boundaries, and deep respect. I often work with women who are confused about why they are unhappy in their families—how can they seem to have it all and still feel so hollow?

The presence of hollowness can be a guide to what needs to change in family systems for the good of the whole. At the same time, family stress is often related to lack of structural safety nets, like healthcare and community support. Either way, the body becomes the focal point of one's efforts to exert control and change, rather than the real causes of stress and pain. Many of the real causes of familial stress are too large for one person to deal with or solve; focusing on the body instead feels like taking control. Meanwhile, the true sources of stress and unhappiness are never truly honored or grieved.

In what ways do you relate to these family patterns of not-quite-enough? What looked like it "should" have been enough, but wasn't or isn't?

Unceasing Growth

In our consumer-based capitalistic culture, we are trained to believe that if we work hard enough and long enough, we will get what we want and need. This deeply held belief in the Western psyche requires us to not stop, never rest, and be in near-constant activity. Social inequities are a stark reminder that this belief is false, yet it's a challenge to resist.

This model of unending growth is indicative of a profound disconnect from the planet, ecological rhythms, and our bodies' natural cycles. When we cannot allow our bodies contraction, rest, and non-doing, we stop breathing deeply, get gripped by anxiety, and, may even experience an existential crisis. Learning to allow for rest and the shedding of what no longer serves us is a move towards increased healthy regulation of ourselves and our lives (as opposed to dysregulation).

How have you experienced pressure to keep going, keep growing, even when it's a season of rest, hibernation, and internal examination? How has this pressure impacted you and your relationship with your soul?

_____

_____

_____

_____

The Nourishment Barrier

When we have been through traumatic, painful, or overwhelming experiences, our bodies can end up getting stuck in a state of fight, flight, or freeze. Fawning is another survival response characterized by people-pleasing and avoidance of conflict to ensure physical or emotional safety. If you have underlying trauma in your nervous system, actually being able to take in nourishment and feel satisfied can be challenging. In order to take in what you need—whether love, food, sexual connection, or nature—your body needs to feel relatively safe. If your body is overly stressed, no matter how surrounded you are by goodness (friends, family, fulfilling work, spiritual practice, and so on), the body cannot register it as nourishing. This phenomenon is called the "nourishment barrier" in somatic psychology. The fawn response and the accompanying nourishment barrier is quite common if you've struggled with body hatred—attuning to the people around you and their needs is possibly a way you've learned to feel safe. As a result, knowing your own needs and taking in what you need can be quite foreign. Learning how to attune to your body, feel your feelings, and access feelings of safety is crucial to being able to take in what we want and need and digest it fully.

What in your life seems like it should be satisfying, but it's not?

_____

_____

_____

_____

As you consider the nourishment barrier, think about the somatic skills you learned in the previous chapter and practice taking in "one drop" at a time. Bring to mind the thing in your life that you named just above as potentially satisfying. What is it like to take in one drop of it? For example, I imagine how in periods of high anxiety in my life, there are moments of calm I often miss. When I slow down and consider the one-drop practice, I think of sitting with a friend and noticing how they are truly listening. I imagine feeling one drop of that connection and care, I notice where I feel it in my body, and I notice how one drop can go a long way towards helping soothe frayed nerves. When you imagine taking in something you're hungry for, what do you notice? Can you feel a change if you slow down and feel one drop at a time?

_____

_____

Take a moment to reflect on the areas in which you might be stuffed-and-starved. Which of these areas resonate the most for you?

_____

_____

Would you add any areas in your life where you feel that focusing on your body is distracting you from a deeper issue?

_____

_____

Many years ago, I was confronted with the stark realization of how stuffed I was with external foci while starved of something deeper. I had accomplished many of my goals, was in a long-term relationship and finally on my own feet financially—and then, Wham! The relationship imploded, necessarily and by my own doing, the job was suddenly suffocating, the work was hollow. One evening, while taking a bath, as I was wont to do as I licked my wounds from heartbreak, I had a clear image of being in the belly of a whale, as in the Biblical myth of Jonah and the whale. The image of Jonah being swallowed by the whale is often interpreted as a spiritual "dark night of the soul" in which there is no clear guiding light, when we must surrender control and do not know what will happen.

I had no idea where I would eventually be spit out—if I ever would be. But my work was to be in the not-knowing, to allow the darkness to envelope me while something changed and morphed deep within me. Eventually I was spit out, quite literally; I moved from New York City to Boulder, Colorado. My life and life focus changed completely to accommodate the psychic shifts that had happened during the dark night in the belly of the unknown. What I had previously been stuffed with was replaced by true nourishment. What I was starved for came rushing in. As is the case with periods of immense upheaval, a new life did emerge on the other side. And in my case, it was more soulful and nourishing than I had known to hope for. I think of this as an encounter with *daimon*—the guiding force that had lowered my tolerance for a relationship already on its last legs made me hope for illness simply to have time off from my stable job and made me aware of how starved I felt for soul and spirit. Facing how stuffed and starved I was, in turn, helped me make courageous and necessary changes toward my soul's path. That's the work of the daimon.

EXERCISE:
"Stuffed-and-Starved"

This journaling practice will help you investigate where you might be stuffed with under-nourishing and depleting tasks, things, and experiences and how you are starved of what you are longing for on a soul level.

Take some time to tune into your body, emotions, and intuition as you begin. Where in your life do you feel stuffed? Where are you overfed, doing too much, or having too much? Is there any-thing in your life that you have so much of that you feel overwhelmed or unable to digest it? For example, this could be excessive screen time, hollow conversations, or an unsatisfying workload. Notice where you have either been given more than you need of something or have simply taken in too much. This is a good way to identify where boundaries are needed as well.

I am stuffed with… _____

_____

_____

I have no more room for… _____

_____

If I have to do/take in/consume _____, I won't be able to take it anymore.

How do you feel, emotionally and physically, as you take stock of this aspect of your life?

_____

_____

_____

_____

Then, identify where in your life you feel starved. Where are you underfed, undernourished? Is there something you are longing for? For some this might be deep connection, time in nature, or having a sense of purpose. Is there something you haven't allowed yourself to have? Is there anything you see other people enjoying that you haven't been able or allowed to access? While this might not change overnight, it's important to name what we need even if we don't immediately receive it.

I am starved of... _____

_____

_____

What I want so deeply it's hard to admit is... _____

_____

If I don't get access to/receive/do _____, my life will feel purposeless, meaningless, untenable.

How do you feel, emotionally and physically, as you notice this aspect of your life?

_____

_____

_____

_____

What I can hear my soul calling for that I don't know how to get is...

_____

_____

_____

_____

After you finish this exercise, you might wonder what to do from here. Maybe you know what you need on a soul level, yet it's absolutely nowhere in sight. So much of what we need on a soul level is not immediately available. It's uncomfortable to realize this. It's counter to consumer culture to need something that we cannot buy. It's so deeply inconvenient to realize we need community when we live in nuclear families. It's so inconvenient to realize we need a change of work when we are strapped financially and have to provide for people we love.

Did this exercise bring up anything inconvenient for you? If so, what are you seeing in your life that is uncomfortable to realize?

_____

_____

_____

It's hard to realize that these deep inconveniences are nurturing to soul. While we might be accustomed, as consumers, to feel a need and have it immediately satisfied, this inconveniencing is, paradoxically, nourishing in an unfamiliar way. It requires that we enter the territory of inconvenience, slow down, and listen to follow a nonlinear path rather than squelch any irritating need by finding a quick fix, which we know will not truly satisfy us.

This place of inconvenience is also where we grieve. Grieve that we don't have what we need on a fundamental level. Grieve that we don't have adequate safety nets. Grieve that what we were sold was woefully inadequate. This grief is a sacred wail that connects us to our calling and purpose—if we can nurture it, feel it, and listen well.

Take Your Eyes Back

When we are connected to soul, the deep and intuitive aspect of ourselves, we feel more centered, more embodied. One way we learn to disconnect from ourselves is by habitually seeing ourselves from the outside-in rather than the inside-out.

Imagine this: You walk into a party and you are immediately aware of being watched. You wonder what people are thinking of you, how they are assessing you. You might wonder if you are you wearing the right thing or moving the right way. You might worry what people think of you, your body, or your behavior. How do you feel? What happens to you when you are thinking that people are watching you? Usually, this is a recipe for social anxiety—unless you really revel in being the center of attention at a party, in which case, this might not be the practice you need! For some people, walking into a party (or meeting or group) is a deeply vulnerable experience because they have internalized the sense of being scrutinized and it makes them self-conscious, resulting in thinking about being seen rather than seeing clearly.

Dynamics of power and privilege can also come into play. Being conscious of being seen is a necessary survival skill, particularly for marginalized groups. Yet it can mean living in survival states rather than reacting from true, embodied connection with ourselves. If we are in the survival state of feeling like prey, alert to being watched, then we might not notice if we are hungry or tired, or how we feel emotionally. If we are focused on being watched, we disconnect from what might be pleasurable and satisfying because we shift to performing rather than relating.

A tool that can help with these dynamics is to take your eyes back. What this skill refers to is being more aware of what you are seeing than you are of being seen, being more aware of who you want to talk to than how you look and more in touch with how you feel than others' possible perceptions of you. In short, this skill can help you undo the habit of being seen instead of seeing from your own eyes, or being desired more than knowing what you desire (or don't desire). This is a skill for being a participant in the world, an agent in it, not an object of the world.

As we discussed in chapter 2, many women learn to objectify themselves. This reflects the impact of the male gaze, a term coined by Laura Mulvey (1975) to describe the way many female figures in media are passive, their identity defined exclusively in relation to male protagonists. The racialized gaze is inherent in this theory—it is white, male protagonists Mulvey refers to. Other feminist scholars have since gone on to write about the ways that women get used to being watched and internalize the male gaze—learning to see ourselves in the objectifying way we're used to being seen—which has far-reaching implications for women's use of voice, agency, and power in the world (Ponterotto 2016).

The dominant masculine cultural gaze (which also tends to be white and heteronormative) disconnects women from their desire, knowing, and intuition. It pulls us out of our bodies as we become trained to see from this internalized gaze rather than from our own eyes. So we need to practice taking our eyes back to see clearly.

To take your eyes back is to practice seeing the world from your own perspective. Do you like the person you're having coffee with? How do you feel in the clothes you're wearing? Are they comfortable? What do you think of the conversation you're overhearing? Do you like the food you're eating? Does it taste good? Taking your eyes back is taking your body back and coming into yourself.

EXERCISE:
Visualization

Get into a comfortable position where you can close your eyes for several minutes and be undisturbed. Imagine walking into a crowded party. You notice that people are looking at you, watching you, seeing you. You can feel people looking at you. What happens in your body? What do you feel emotionally? Notice if you enjoy this experience, or contract in it: are you feeling anxious, or do you have a desire to withdraw or hide?

Then, rewind your imagination. Re-enter this crowded party and imagine that you now are the one doing the looking, the seeing. You walk in and while some heads turn to notice you, you also notice them. You take in your surroundings. You notice what people are wearing. You notice the vibe, the feel of the room. You notice how you feel in the room. You may feel anxious, but you take the anxiety with you as you keep walking. Maybe you also feel curious, or just neutral. Finally, *you* choose where to go next, based on to whom you are drawn.

Did you notice a difference between the two scenes? Did you feel anything different in your body or about your body? What was it like to imagine being seen versus doing the seeing?

_____

_____

_____

_____

_____

EXERCISE:
Seeing Clearly

Pick a day this coming week to practice. On this day, simply notice what you see, what you feel, and what your perspective on particular situations is. When you notice yourself moving into self-objectification, consider these questions as a practice for taking back your eyes, re-embodying your unique self, perspective, and judgments:

- What do I see? How do I feel about what I'm seeing?

- What am I hearing? Do I agree or disagree with a perspective I'm hearing?

- What do I think and feel about this situation?

- Do I like or dislike what is happening?

At the end of the day, reflect:

At which times in the day were you especially clear about your feelings and opinions?

_____

_____

At which times in the day were you especially unconscious of your own feelings and opinions?

_____

_____

What was it like to deliberately shift *out* of self-objectification, or to shift from unconscious passage through your own life to conscious habitation of a given moment? Were you able to do it successfully, or was it a struggle?

_____

_____

Remember that being self-aware is important to survival and societal maneuvering. This exercise is not intended to diminish the real skill and necessity of navigating the environment of complex social situations with regard to how you do or don't fit into it in a given moment, or moments when you might need to adjust to or accommodate others, particularly when differences of power and privilege are at play. But bringing your own awareness of where you stand in relation to others and to your own experience and authenticity to consciousness can help you to move from internalized objectification into external skillful maneuvering.

The 80/20 Practice

This practice can be done in any setting, but is particularly effective in social situations, especially if you feel like you "merge" with your surroundings and have a hard time staying connected to your body, feelings, or even your own thoughts. In this context, merging refers to the experience of being so alert and aware to what's happening and to the people around you that you lose a sense of your own individuality and awareness—you might know what others are feeling but have no idea what you are feeling. You might know what others need but be disconnected from your needs.

Imagine that you have millions of tiny antennae that act like radar. Your antennae can be tuned outward, to your surroundings and people; tuned inward to your feelings and body sensations; or both. When people struggle with body hatred, most of these antennae are tuned outward, picking up on other people's feelings, moods, and needs. Imagine that 100% of your antennae are tuned outward. What does that mean? It means that no one is really "home"—no one is tracking if you're tired, angry, or even hungry. This is a normal state for people who grew up in chaotic homes, for instance—it's always safer to know who's walking into the room, even which mood is entering the room, than to be connected to our own needs. But as adults, or outside the settings in which this sort of vigilance is necessary, this skill loses its utility.

Now imagine 100% of your antennae being tuned inward. This could be equally problematic—you'd be vulnerable, easily caught unaware of anything happening externally.

In recovery from body hatred, to come back into our bodies we practice holding attention inwards and outwards, making fine adjustments as we do this. The way I do this with clients is to have them imagine their antennae tuned all the way out and then all the way in. Then I have them move to a 50/50 split, then a 75/25 split in favor of the inward, and then an 80/20 split. With the 80/20 split, most of our attention is on our own experience and the data this gives us, the insight into what we truly feel and need—while we devote just enough attention to the outside to ensure we're appropriately conscious of it. Disproportionate attention to the outside keeps us reactive and stuck in fear, insecurity, shame, or unconsciousness of ourselves.

EXERCISE:
The 80/20 Practice

Take a moment to experiment with this yourself.

What do you notice with 100% of your antennae tuned outwards? And how about with 100% of your antennae tuned inwards?

_____

_____

_____

_____

_____

Is there an "ideal" inwards/outwards ratio that feels good to your body? How does 80/20 feel to you?

_____

_____

_____

_____

_____

_____

In the end, 80/20 may not be the right balance for you. If not, I encourage you to find the balance that does feel right. Ultimately, the purpose of this practice is to start to inhabit your body more fully, to take up embodied space, which means being in tune with your body and your inner world.

Again, inhabiting your body is necessary for recovering from body hatred. It's harder to hate your body when you are in tune with it—instead, compassion, curiosity, and care for your body tend to develop. It's also how you listen to soul: by tuning inwards and feeling carefully.

Connecting to Soul: Nature Listening and Dreamwork

When we are talking about soul and the *anima mundi*, it's hard to avoid the fact that western psychology has largely de-animated nature and has a dismissive attitude toward dreams. Relating to nature as a concrete external practice and working with our dreams are largely omitted from evidence-based therapies. But these are two direct pathways for learning how to listen more deeply to your soul and the soul of the world in all their mysteriousness.

Going into nature is often recommended for self-care and personal healing, which it certainly can offer. But from a depth psychological perspective, engaging with the natural world is to recognize that the natural world *acts on us* and we *act on it*—it is not a passive amusement park for the human senses, it is alive and animate. To engage with soul, one of the most foundational and impactful experiences you can have is to go outside and really *be in it*. Be blown around by the wind. Feel your body react to the temperature change, the movement of the air, the smells. Sometimes in body hatred recovery, the hardest thing people can learn to do is to go outside without the agenda to exercise—so when you go out, try to do so without the intention to exercise. Go outside just to feel the wind, for instance. Listen to the wind; feel it acting upon you and you upon it. Consider relating to the wind, being with it as though it was also alive.

When I was in the thick of my doctoral dissertation, I hit the end of my capacities. I was bone-tired from parenting a new baby during the pandemic, working full-time, and writing my dissertation early in the mornings. The absolute last thing I wanted to do was read through and organize the interviews that my research participants had so generously given to me. One day I was lamenting to myself about how maybe I would not finish my PhD; I would just call it a day and move on with my life. I held a personal ceremony of sorts, asking for guidance around this situation and for a new vision to help me move forward. What happened during this ceremony was a direct confrontation with something deeper inside that said, "A new vision? What in the world are you going to do with a new vision? You have people's sacred body stories in your hands—be grateful, honor what you've been given, and do something with those stories!" I got the point—I didn't need a new vision, I needed to re-engage with the sacredness of what was right in front of me.

The next day I bought a bouquet of flowers to honor all the stories I received in my research process. I went to the river by my house and made a mandala of flowers for each story and participant and, with all the reverence I could muster, asked for support from the river to finish my dissertation well. Then I got back to work. I did eventually finish writing the dissertation, and that research led to this book you're holding in your hands. This is one example of how I have personally engaged with ceremony and nature to find my way through a hard life moment. Since I don't come from a culture where nature-based ceremonies are common, my attempts are usually clumsy and always imperfect. Yet I can count on feeling more human and connected to something more lasting as a result of my attempts. You can try this for yourself in the exercise that follows.

EXERCISE:
Nature Listening

Find a place outside you can go and pause for a few moments. This can be anywhere, including a sidewalk bench, a beach, or your own porch. You'll need to be able to be still for several minutes, so choose a place that will allow that. Bring an offering of some kind that is biodegradable (flowers, leaves, or food that won't harm the wildlife) or find something beautiful on your way. When you arrive, place your offering on the ground and, in your own way, say thank you to nature. Take three deep breaths and settle into your body.

Consider a question about your life you are holding. In what area of your life do you want guidance? Where are you needing insight? If you have a question for the larger, guiding force of nature, what might it be?

_____

_____

_____

_____

Imagine that rather than thinking of a response, you pause long enough to truly listen. Listen to the wind, notice the light around you, take in what's happening through your senses. Breathe.

Now ask yourself: If the aspects of nature around you are saying something, what do you hear?

_____

_____

_____

_____

If the wind, earth, light, or plants around you have a response to your question, what is it?

_____

_____

_____

_____

In response, if you have a message for nature, what is it? How might you express that message in your own way?

Take some time to reflect on this experience. What do you feel after engaging with nature in this way? How do you want to move forward with your day as a result?

_____

_____

_____

_____

_____

_____

_____

_____

Dreamwork

Dreams are the interface between our conscious and unconscious selves. Dreams are the untamed territory that cannot be controlled by conscious will, like wild animals that we cannot get away from no matter how civilized we consider ourselves to be. They persist, untouched by our attempts to control them, offering glimpses into the depths of our inner world. In this way, dreams provide profound insight into the aspects of ourselves that are hidden during waking hours.

If you ask five people what dreams are, you will get five different answers. There isn't much consensus about why we dream, what the purpose of dreams is, and what to do with the mysterious world that visits us at night. A neuroscientist might explain that dreams are simply the haphazard firings of the brain, trying to synthesize information after a long day, while a behaviorist might say that dreams are our attempts at solving problems we don't know how to solve. The Jungian perspective is that dreams are direct experiences with the unconscious; they are living, real aspects of psyche that have the potential to direct our lives from the level of soul, if we engage with them with attention and respect. Dreams are one way we listen to the guiding force of the *daimon*, yet very few of us have received guidance on how to work with the complex language of dreams.

SYMBOLISM VS. LITERALISM

In a dream, we often experience people, places, and objects that are familiar to us. In a dream, these familiar images are not literally who or what they are in waking life, although those of us who are unfamiliar with working with symbols might mistake these symbolic experiences for literal ones. Because I am familiar with symbolic language, if I dream about my brother, I consider what my brother represents. I do not interpret my dream as being about my actual brother (although this is not a hard-and-fast rule). Another way to put this is that my dream chose my brother to show me something that I associate my brother with. In dreamwork we shift from seeing images literally to seeing them symbolically. There is a deeper meaning and essence to the images in our dreams, and we have to learn to listen with flexibility and curiosity.

DREAM IMAGES AS PARTS OF YOU

One way to work with dreams is to consider every part of the dream—objects, people, even sounds—as aspects of you. For example, during a period of recovery from heartbreak and betrayal by a loved one, I worked with a dream in which this person had a new body piercing. In my dreamwork process, I embodied the image of the piercing—I imagined *being* the piercing, suspending my sense of self, my mind, and its interpretations. I realized that I felt so hurt that I wanted to "pierce" this person. In other words, this image helped me contact my anger and aggression without acting it out unconsciously or in person. It also helped me move through my heartache more consciously. When we work with dream images as parts of ourselves, then we practice embodying the image and hearing from it directly.

BALANCING THE PSYCHE

Dreams balance our conscious, waking mind with the unconscious, nonlinear, and nonrational aspects of the psyche. In Jungian terms, dreams are considered compensatory and confirming—they compensate by showing us something we need to see, feel, or acknowledge, and they confirm by highlighting something we might be minimizing in our lives. Our cultural belittlement of dreams, our tendency to see them as alternately fun or annoying fantasies our brains just happen to produce, reflects a loss of symbolic thinking and appreciation for the unconscious and soul. Dreamwork is one powerful way to come into contact with soul, the *daimon*, and deeper emotions that have been suppressed through the turmoil of body hatred, particularly as that turmoil begins to be cleared in favor of something deeper.

Here are some suggestions for working with your dreams over the weeks to come.

1. If you don't remember your dreams regularly, start by waking up more slowly in the morning—when your alarm goes off, pause. Delay scrolling on your phone or hopping out of bed. You are mostly likely having dreams, but not remembering them. Waking up slowly and intending to remember helps bridge the realms of dreamtime and daytime.

2. Keep a journal or pad of paper of your dreams by the side of your bed. This signals to psyche you're interested in what your dreams have to say. As soon as you wake, try to write down anything you remember before even getting out of bed. (You can also use the voice notes app on your phone if you prefer.)

3. When you write a dream down, write it in first-person, present tense: "I am in a boat with my dog. We are headed to a party." Journaling is helpful to track themes that we otherwise tend to miss over time.

4. Actively work with at least one dream a week using the dream worksheet below.

5. Make a ritual out of your dream—meaning, don't just sit there with the insight you're getting; do something! Toni Wolfe, a revered Jungian analyst, used to send her clients away if they hadn't taken their dream seriously enough to do something physical or material about them. She would tell them they weren't ready for the work she was offering if they had only thought about their dreams. I'll go with Toni here and say, if you've taken the time to remember your dreams, write them down, and explore them, then do something tangible as well. Change a behavior, write a letter, try something new.

EXERCISE:
Dreamwork

Dream: Write your dream in the first person and present tense. For example, "I'm walking down my street, but it's a different street than my waking one. I sense someone with me."

_____

_____

_____

_____

What did you feel in the dream? How did you feel upon waking? Do you have any intuitions about this dream?

_____

_____

_____

Write any questions you have about your dream.

_____

_____

_____

_____

Choose three images from your dream that have energy—these can be a person, object, or place in your dream. Which images caught your attention? Which ones were vivid or confusing? Write down the three images you are going to work with for this exercise.

_____

_____

_____

Now, take your time imagining becoming each image—feel it from the inside out. Trust yourself, and simply play with what you hear and notice. For example, if I choose a boat as one of my dream images, here's what I would do: I feel into the boat, as though it's alive, as though I am the boat. As the boat, I answer the questions on the worksheet: "I am a place of refuge. I float when everything else is sinking. I'm here to take people to a safe place."

Dream Image 1	
Who am I?	
Why am I here?	
What do I want the dreamer to know?	
What guidance do I have for the dreamer?	

Dream Image z	
Who am I?	
Why am I here?	
What do I want the dreamer to know?	
What guidance do I have for the dreamer?	

Dream Image 3	
Who am I?	
Why am I here?	
What do I want the dreamer to know?	
What guidance do I have for the dreamer?	

Take time to reflect on these images and what came forward from them. What was this dream about?

_____

_____

_____

_____

_____

_____

Why is it relevant for your life today?

_____

_____

_____

_____

What are you carrying forward from this dream?

_____

_____

_____

_____

If you'd like to continue working with your dreams this way, you'll find a worksheet for this exercise at http://www.newharbinger.com/52076.

Being willing to work with your dreams often requires a leap of faith. When I ask clients to bring in a dream to support our work, it usually takes a few nudges for them to finally bring one in. Usually, the dream offers a missing piece to our work together. Sometimes, the dream is life-changing—not because the dream itself was dramatic or striking in some way, but because the dream held a piece of feeling or knowledge that was unconscious and now is conscious, as all dreams do. Dreams are the humble, ever-present guides that we so easily dismiss, like the ants in the myth of Psyche and Eros we explored in chapter 3. Ever-present, yet minimized.

Body hatred and attempts to change our bodies are a clear example of the "concretization of the psyche," which means that rather than looking at our pain, turmoil, and longing for a different body symbolically, we act it out concretely.

In your body hatred recovery journey, shifting from the tangible to the symbolic is a vital task. Rather than concretizing all your personal hopes into the shape or size of your body, you are learning to work with these longings symbolically, which is what dreamwork can help you learn to do.

Conclusion

As we reach the end of this book, consider: how are you feeling towards your body? Perhaps you've reached the point at which body hatred and how you feel about your body is less of a focus than the question of what nourishes you, what fulfills you, what brings you closer to your purpose, and how you can have more of that. Or maybe you're still struggling with body hatred, and you're at the point where persistence and patience are called for.

No matter where you find yourself, there usually comes a time when fighting your body becomes too much to bear. The fight is too tiring, the effort too much for so little in return. This state of fatigue and frustration can lead to a phase of feeling so done with the struggle that something else is allowed to emerge. While this phase, which I call the "inner conflict" phase, can persist for years, the change of path and the change of mind that emerge are deep and foundational. Theresa described this fertile frustration as motivating deeper change with her body: "I just really decided that I didn't want to be on the roller coaster anymore. It was exhausting—I would swing between deprivation and then wanting to eat because I was deprived. And I didn't want to do it anymore." The "swing" between the poles of self-hate and deprivation to fatigue and giving in express the exhaustion that you may feel when your relationship with your body is at a breaking point.

In depth psychology, this inner conflict between your body and how you feel about your body is an example of the "tension of opposites" that, if you can tolerate and work with it, can lead to a new psychological stage and inner perspective. This stable, internalized change of perspective is possible because of what Jung called the "transcendent function," which is birthed out of frustration and inner conflict. It is the experience of transforming from one state and becoming able to see something else entirely (Jung 1958/1969).

Trying to change your attitude toward your body can be cyclical, like a merry-go-round that never fully stops. It looks like this: *I wake up hating my body and decide to do something about it. I start to make a change. The change is unsustainable—life gets in the way, or old patterns reassert themselves—so I fail. I feel shame that I can't sustain it. I feel numb towards my body for a while. Then, eventually, I wake up and hate my body once again…* And so it continues. That is, until something breaks through consciousness—a moment of epiphany or an external experience that breaks you out of the cycle. For Cynthia, what broke her out of this cycle was a cancer diagnosis that made her confront her mortality. For others, the change can appear more mundane, a moment of awareness when you hear an inner voice say, "I can't do this anymore" or "I'm just so tired…" or "I want something else." These moments serve the psychological function of making deeper needs and feelings conscious, which is a primary task of becoming more yourself. For still others, the process of moving out of frustration and back into lasting change can be a task they deliberately recommit themselves to, time and time again, until finally the transcendent function comes into play.

If you persist, you'll find that the struggle with food, body, and purpose is an initiatory process. It is often a journey from unconsciousness to consciousness, from adolescent obedience and rebellion to mature adulthood and knowing why you are here.

Initiation: Becoming Adult

Once I asked a woman who had largely recovered from an eating disorder and body hatred why she thought she had been through such a struggle. After a long pause, she replied, "I wanted to go through something dark." That's the language of initiation—of the difficult experiences we go through as rituals to achieve some deeper understanding. And this woman had wanted to go through *something dark*. Of course, this wasn't conscious for her at the time—it rarely is. This may not resonate for you; you may not feel your struggle with body hatred as something you willed to happen, consciously or not, to any degree. Yet often, the soul pulls us into dark places to reach maturity and integration.

Integration, in depth psychology, refers most specifically to shadow integration—*shadow* being the parts of ourselves that we deny or disown because they are somehow unacceptable to us or the society we inhabit. Shadow aspects includes our impulses, desires, or insecurities that conflict with who we see ourselves as, who we want to be, or who we are seen to be by others. *Integration* in this sense refers to making these parts conscious, accepting them, and working with them in a way that leads to increase wholeness. And initiation into adulthood, which is almost always marked by going through something hard, shows us what we are made of and what is true for us; it requires that we go into the darkness of the underworld to reclaim the gifts of the psyche.

In the initiation journey that is recovery from body hatred, we cannot look to mass culture for guidance. We must look for the elders, those who've gone before us: the women who know how to live respectfully in their bodies, who have a critical eye on the lies we are often fed about what it means to be a powerful woman or person; those who hold their wisdom close and know how important their intuition is. Sometimes these wisdom keepers fly under the radar. These people are unlikely to be banging the drum of body positivity; they probably inhabit their bodies with a different, hard-won kind of confidence and intensity.

EXERCISE:
Finding a Guide

To help you move through this initiation, see if you can identify one person in your life who is comfortable in their body, despite ability, health, or size. If there isn't such a person in your life you can think of in this way, imagine someone.

Think of or imagine someone who could be a kind of model for body peace for you.

_____

_____

_____

Look closely. Watch how this person moves through the world. How do they use their voice? What is their relationship with their body like? How do they feed themselves? Reflect on how this person, or your ideal image of such a person, moves through the world.

_____

_____

_____

_____

_____

_____

_____

Initiation's Phases

As you read through the following phases of an initiation journey focused on recovery from body hatred, notice where you feel resonance. Notice where you feel a lack of energy. Your reactions can point to where you are in your own journey. Since we are at the end of this book and you've learned and practiced new skills along the way, you may already be in one of the later phases. In that case, I suggest answering those questions by considering how you want to live your life moving forward rather than how you've lived it up to this point.

Phase 1: Obedience

Obedience is the first phase of the journey. In this phase, you follow the established norms and conventions of family and culture, often unaware of your own inner wisdom and desires. Obedience is an important part of our childhood development; we learn how to be in the world in which we find ourselves by following rules and expectations set by others. And this includes, of course, how we relate to and feel about our bodies. This stage can persist into adulthood and limit our deepening into ourselves. Additionally, this phase is characterized by feeling separate from your body, as though your body is a problem to solve or a kind of burden to bear. The end of this phase is often marked by questioning these norms.

Markers of the Obedience Phase

- Following societal norms and expectations, particularly around your body

- Chronic and persistent attempts to alter and control your body

- Feeling content but disconnected from your body and deep self

GUIDING QUESTIONS

What are the rules and expectations I have followed in my life? What are the rules I've followed regarding how I treat my body?

_____

_____

_____

_____

What parts of me have I been suppressing in order to fit into these norms and expectations?

_____

_____

How have these norms and expectations impacted my relationship with my body?

_____

_____

Phase 2: Inner Conflict

The second phase, inner conflict, marks the beginning of an emotional stirring, where we start to ask deeper questions about our happiness, fulfillment, and purpose in life. We start to feel a pull to a different way. A subtle inner spark starts to wake up. Nothing is wrong exactly, but we have a sense that something is shifting within us and a change is needed. It might start with questions like, "Does it actually have to be this hard to maintain my body?" or "Why am I working so hard on this diet again?"

In this phase the old ways of coping, dieting (in all its forms), or living in your body start to fail. Previous coping strategies no longer protect against deeper emotions. As discussed earlier, frustration serves an important purpose by heightening a sense of dissatisfaction that can lead to more concrete life changes, but the phase of frustration is distinct. You might start to feel afraid that your life is about to fall apart...or even have a strange sense that you want it to fall apart in some way. This can be a vulnerable and confusing time, but it is also a crucial step in the journey toward body peace.

It is still easy to get off the train here and retreat from changes that lie ahead, which is why it is such an important moment—it can lead to change or not. You may be able to cope fairly easily by trying a new exercise class, or making a resolution to shift your mindset, or embark on a new health regimen. But these could be temporary fixes in the larger process of learning how to relate respectfully to your body.

Markers of the Inner Conflict Phase:

- The experience of feeling lost, stuck, or unfulfilled

- The realization that the old ways of coping, dealing, and being are no longer working

- A breaking down of the old self, leading to a deeper search for meaning and purpose

GUIDING QUESTIONS

What function is my frustration serving? What is it trying to tell me?

_____

_____

What are the beliefs and attitudes I have been carrying that are no longer serving me?

_____

_____

What is the inner wisdom that I have been suppressing, and how can I listen to it more deeply?

_____

_____

Phase 3: Crisis

The third phase of the body peace journey is crisis, or the dark night of the soul, characterized by a crescendo of emotion and a sense of chaos as you navigate your life. It's when stuff starts to hit the fan. This is a phase in which life changes dramatically. It's not exactly fun or pleasant or entertaining, but it is often necessary to begin to let go, surrender, and listen to your deeper needs and desires. The dark night of the soul often occurs when we realize we can no longer do it alone and, if we try to muscle it out by ourselves, we could dig ourselves deeper into a hole. For some people, this crisis phase looks like an internal crisis—anxiety that turns into panic attacks or sadness that moves into depression. Or it can be external: a cheating spouse, a bad review at work, a lost job, or the death of a loved one, for example.

These experiences of crisis can range from traumatic to epiphanic—traumatic being something happening from the outside that you feel unable to cope with, and epiphanic being a psychological or mental breaking through of insight. These crisis experiences lead to external changes that can no longer be avoided—a move, a career change, starting therapy, beginning or ending a relationship, and more. The crisis period is when the shell around our inner wisdom gets cracked open. And as inconvenient as it is, a broken heart is often what allows us to tap into soul and true hunger.

Markers of Crisis:

- Dramatic change—internally or externally in your life

- The letting go of everything that is no longer needed or wanted

- The experience of feeling vulnerable and alone, as though the old life has fundamentally changed, but the new one has not yet arrived

GUIDING QUESTIONS

What beliefs, values, and parts of my identity do I need to let go of?

_____

_____

_____

How can I surrender control and trust in the journey ahead?

_____

_____

How can I find solace and peace during this challenge?

_____

_____

Phase 4: Opening of Mind

The fourth phase of this journey is opening of mind. After a crisis of trauma or a numinous moment of awareness, the mind opens to new information. The opening of mind phase is characterized by self-reflection and sorting through your internal world, including your beliefs, thoughts, feelings, and memories. The importance of a mentor and new community during this phase, to guide and offer support as you find your way to a new life path, cannot be overstated. This phase is marked by a cognitive and emotional opening to learn and integrate new information, leading to a new understanding of life.

In this phase, you are ripe for education. You need it, you are hungry for it. And during this phase, there is often a sense of synchronicity with whatever might cross your path; you might feel you've found the right book at the right time, a new mentor or therapist, a friend who is suddenly considering the same ideas you are, and more. Essentially, this is a time of fertility of mind. Allow the opening of your mind to be fed by good, healthy information and sources. In this phase, you might need to limit social media and avoid people who are still stuck in body hatred and diet culture for a time. Find what feeds you on the deepest level and eat it up.

Markers of Opening of Mind:

- A process of self-reflection and sorting through your internal world

- A mentor and new community serve as guides to a new life path

- Cognitive and emotional opening to learn and integrate new information

GUIDING QUESTIONS

What is the dominant belief I was taught about my body that I'm wanting to transform now?

_____

_____

Who can serve as a mentor or guide to help me on my journey toward a new understanding of life and my body?

_____

_____

What new information or options for living life in a new way am I open to exploring and integrating?

_____

_____

_____

Phase 5: Sensing the Body

Sensing the body in the phase in which you reconnect with yourself—your feelings, desires, and body. The phase of learning to sense your body is a crucial one in the body hatred recovery. As we discussed in the fourth chapter, you develop a connection to your body by feeling and attuning to it rather than thinking about and controlling it. Sensing the body involves making somatic contact with the body, which is vital for accessing information, facilitating inner healing, and experiencing pleasure. This phase is characterized by your mind following the needs of your body rather than your body being subservient to your mind. This is a step toward the next phase of embodiment.

This stage can lead to life-altering experiences as you discover parts of yourself you never knew existed and start to connect with the world in a deeper way. As you reconnect with your body, you might reconnect with feelings, dreams, desires, grief, and unmet hunger. The blessing of this period is that once you connect more with your body and deeper desires and needs, you start to connect with the world in a deeper way. Your interests might start changing. You might start to prefer staying home to nights out. You might prefer to read a book that is way outside of your comfort zone. You might notice that you need more rest or more movement. This is an interesting, ongoing phase of listening to the body with care and attunement, which connects us to the deeper longings of soul.

Markers of Sensing the Body

- Developing inner connection to your body through somatic contact

- The mind following the body rather than the body being subservient to the mind

- Accessing information, facilitating inner healing, and experiencing pleasure through your body

GUIDING QUESTIONS

How do I feel my body from the inside out rather than thinking about it with my mind?

_____

_____

What is preventing me from making somatic (felt, physical) contact with my body?

_____

_____

If my body could speak to me, what would it say?

_____

_____

Phase 6: Integration and Stability

The sixth phase of making peace with the body is the integration and stability phase. This phase is characterized by a stable and consistent relationship with your body and a sense of arrival. Aspects of this phase include feeling engaged with your life's purpose now that your body isn't your main project, using your voice effectively, and feeling a sense of relief over finding a different way of living that is more aligned with your true calling. After you break yourself down and reassemble yourself anew, life begins again. In the integration and stability phase, you can see that you've started to integrate and embody all the new changes that you've experienced. It's the phase in which all of your hard-won wisdom comes into play and allows you to be of service to the world.

Markers of Integration and Stability

- Feeling aligned with your purpose, less distracted by body preoccupation or body hatred

- Understanding the generational meaning of making peace with your body—how changing your relationship with your body affects more than just yourself

- Emanating from your body rather than performing

GUIDING QUESTIONS

How is your life different now that you feel more at peace with your body?

_____

_____

_____

How has engaging with your life purpose impacted your relationship with your body?

_____

_____

What role has using your voice played in your journey towards body peace? How do you relate to boundaries now?

_____

_____

_____

Phase 7: Growth Edges

Integration and stability may seem like the end, but in reality, there is no end. Phase 7, the growth edges phase, honors the fact that we are never complete; the journey we're on in life is not linear, but a spiral, one that keeps turning as long as we're alive. For some people, learning how to exercise without attaching to weight loss or being vigilant of the ways body shame can easily sneak back in, no matter how recovered they might be, are ongoing challenges for body peace. For others, an initial period of body respect is followed by a resurgence of internalized shame about the body or in other areas of identity. This is normal and is part of psyche's ongoing journey toward wholeness. I call this phase "growth edges" because it's about the experience of realizing how you need to change and grow despite all your progress so far. Growth edges are the places you're stretching yourself and your comfort zone, which requires tolerating the distress of making long-term changes over and over again.

For example, many people think that body respect or body peace equals loving one's body. But they are not the same. For one thing, respect goes beyond the positive. Most people I work with who feel at peace with their bodies are more neutral or appreciative, rather than overtly positive about their bodies; they still cope with ongoing criticisms of their bodies, from themselves and from others. It is the ability to cope and move through these thoughts, rather than reacting to them by disconnecting from the body or punishing it, that demonstrates the more stable psychological change that has occurred. To remain conscious of deep cultural and familial conditioning requires continual effort, recommitment, and maintenance. Ultimately, seeing growth edges as a distinct phase of the journey helps us maintain the on-going self-awareness that's needed to practice body respect, particularly as our bodies age and inevitably diminish, despite all the promises of ever-present youth in larger culture.

Markers of Growth Edges

- Ongoing engagement with new aspects of the journey to make peace with the body

- Nonlinear process that requires ongoing self-reflection and exploration of new growth edges

- Finding new areas of the self to explore, change, and heal

GUIDING QUESTIONS

How can I push my growth edges and learn through experimentation and new experiences?

_____

_____

How can I be of service to the world with all I have to offer?

_____

_____

How can I cultivate deeper connections with my community and the world around me?

_____

_____

In reflecting on these phases, where are you in this journey?

_____

_____

_____

_____

Growing up, I didn't have a lot of models of adult women who were secure in their own skin. Most of the people who were tasked with raising me struggled with their bodies and were on weird diets most of the time. When it was my time to take up the mantle of body preoccupation and body hatred, I resented the psychological explanations and diagnoses for why and how I struggled with my body. I was simply following the old order that no one ever named because it was so familiar, normal, and natural.

As a clinician, I now know that the old explanations and diagnoses for eating disorders and body dysmorphia are deeply inadequate; poor recovery rates echo this inadequacy. As I was growing up, swimming in the water of socialized female body hatred, no one ever mentioned culture being a problem; no one ever mentioned sexism being an issue. My body problem was first and foremost a personal problem. I now know this is rarely the case.

I eventually found my way to soulful, wise practitioners who held my hand as I faced the challenging reality of living in a culture that is deeply disconnected from soul, earth, and care for people and began my own initiation—facing reality, feeling grief, making changes. In my recovery, I had to take some big risks, challenging my usual hyperresponsible, hyperpractical modus operandus in order to get in line with my calling and deep self. To make real change I had to make real, consequential changes. These changes were the result of my own initiatory process, the journey of going through something dark to be changed and to make change. I encourage you to make brave changes, go deep, and trust that a different way is possible.

Body Peace as Individual and Systemic

In this book, I have provided you with guidance for your own journey to body peace. On this journey you learned, first, to identify and discard all the internalized messages about your body that you have inherited from culture, media, and family. Then you learned how to identify where the ideas about your body came from and systematically weed them out of you. You will need to keep doing this on a consistent basis since external, systemic change is slow to occur.

But if you can do this, you will eventually become yourself, be yourself, and embody yourself to your edges You will know that you've succeeded when you feel your feelings, when you pay attention to your intuition as part of yourself, when you respect yourself, when you shine your gifts into the world, when you let your body take up space, when you honor the reality that from the moment you were born, you deserved to be here, and act accordingly.

Then you can start to find places to effect change for others so they can feel safer and more at peace in their bodies. You may do this through small demonstrations of treating your own body respectfully all the way to more socially oriented change actions such as advocating for respectful treatment of all bodies on a political level. Shifting our orientation from individually based action to systemic change is vital to create more nurturing cultures for our bodies.

These are the three essential steps in the journey to feeling and being at peace with your body. The first step is usually the easiest. The second step—the spiritual, emotional process of becoming a person in a body with purpose and worth—is harder. It's how you make an essential shift from performing yourself to emanating yourself: from striving to embody some ideal you hold to simply being yourself, inside your skin, connected to your feelings, and rooted in your soma, your body.

The third step of making systemic, social change is not necessarily the last. Yet I consider it a foundational issue: we need cultural change to feel more peaceful within our bodies. Focusing on individual change is often a distraction from the larger cultural problems that impact our internal experience of our bodies. But I understand that when we feel at war with our body, it's hard to shift into effective external actions. On the journey to make peace with our bodies, eventually we come to see that social, cultural change is the real need. It is my hope that during our recovery journeys, we can come to find our place within that larger process, no matter how subtle or vibrant our activism appears to be.

Walking the Initiated Path

I have a hypothesis that people who hate their bodies or struggle with eating disorders are deeply intuitive people. In my work with women recovering from body hatred, often we hit the ground of grief that is where seeds of body hatred were planted and sprouted and grew. The ground of grief is bigger than any individual life; it's often related to cultural gaps—lack of community, lack of true spiritual guidance, and the poverty of a culture that has forgotten to teach its subjects how to do basic things like take care of one another, take care of ourselves, reflect, eat well, and rest. I don't know if there was a past utopia in which humans lived harmoniously and with care for their people and place, but still, it's quite clear that the contemporary cultures you and I have been exposed to have forgotten such things. And I think we sense this— we sense that we are living ultimately unsustainable lives. Body hatred is a convenient out-growth of a culture that has forgotten how to truly be in respectful relationship with where we live. It makes sense to me that if we don't know how to be in relationship with our planet, then we don't quite know how to be in respectful relationship with our bodies. We are in respectful relationships when we honor limits, when we acknowledge that everything has a death on the horizon so this moment means something, and when we realize we aren't the only game in town—that maybe our needs and ambitions aren't everything. Other people and other-than-human beings also have a life to live; it might be wise to consider the impact of our ambitions on them. Psychologically, this is the process of individuation—we become less self-centric and more soul-centric, which connects us to the reality of our interdependence with other people, places, and other-than-human beings.

To be in respectful relationship with our bodies means that we begin to honor the limits of our bodies. We cannot exercise at forty the way we did at twenty without some serious consequences. We cannot expect our bodies to endure calorie restriction in whatever form without facing the consequences in our older years. And the consequences of focusing on hating our bodies rather than looking at the culture that instilled this hatred in us will also be felt more with age. So, I conclude this book with a plea to you to not allow body hatred to dictate how you spend the rest of your days. You have much more important work to do, and the world needs you to do it.

Recommended Reading to Continue Your Journey

Reclaiming Body Trust: A Path to Healing and Liberation by Hilary Kinavey and Dana Sturtevant

The Body is Not an Apology by Sonya Renee Taylor

Body Respect: What Conventional Health Books Get Wrong, Leave Out, and Just Plain Fail to Understand about Weight by Linda Bacon and Lucy Aphramor

Pleasure Activism by adrienne maree brown

Care Work: Dreaming Disability Justice by Leah Lakshmi Piepzna-Samarasinha

What We Don't Talk About When We Talk About Fat by Aubrey Gordon

Fearing the Black Body: The Racial Origins of Fat Phobia by Sabrina Strings

Radical Acceptance: Embracing Your Life with the Heart of a Buddha by Tara Brach

Eating in the Light of the Moon: How Women Can Transform Their Relationship with Food Through Myths, Metaphors, and Storytelling by Anita Johnston

Anti-Diet by Christy Harrison

References

Bartky, S. 1990. *Femininity and Domination: Studies in the Phenomenology of Oppression.* New York: Routledge Press.

Bordo, S. 2003. *Unbearable Weight: Feminism, Western Culture, and the Body.* Los Angeles: University of California Press.

Brumberg, J. J. 1998. *The Body Project: An Intimate History of American Girls.* New York: Vintage Books.

Erskine, R. 1998. "Attunement and Involvement: Therapeutic Responses to Relational Needs." *International Journal of Psychotherapy* 3: 235–244.

Estés, C. P. 1992. *Women Who Run with the Wolves: Myths and Stories of the Wild Woman Archetype.* New York: Ballantine Books.

Farrell, A. E. 2011. *Fat Shame: Stigma and the Fat Body in American Culture.* New York: New York University Press.

Fredrickson, B., and T.-A. Roberts. 1997. "Objectification Theory: Toward Understanding Women's Lived Experiences and Mental Health Risks." *Psychology of Women Quarterly* 21: 173–206. https://doi.org/10.1111/j.1471-6402.1997.tb00108.x.

Fuller, C. 2017. *The Fat Lady Sings: A Psychological Exploration of the Cultural Fat Complex and Its Effects.* London: Karnac Books.

Gay, R. K., and E. Castano. 2010. "My Body or My Mind: The Impact of State and Trait Objectification on Women's Cognitive Resources." *European Journal of Social Psychology* 40: 695–703. https://doi.org/10.1002/ejsp.731.

Grabe, S., and J. S. Hyde. 2009. "Body Objectification, MTV, and Psychological Outcomes among Female Adolescents." *Journal of Applied Social Psychology* 39: 2840–2858. https://doi.org/10.1111/j.1559-1816.2009.00552.x.

Gutwill, S. 2018. "Toward Social Justice: The Continuum of Eating and Body Image Problems: How Social and Psychological Realities Converge into an Embodied Epidemic." In *Psychoanalytic Treatment of Eating Disorders: When Words Fail and Bodies Speak*, edited by T. Wooldridge, 241–267. London: Routledge.

Hillman, J. 1996. *The Soul's Code: In Search of Character and Calling*. New York: Warner Books.

Jung, C. G. 1969. "The Transcendent Function." Translated by R. F. C. Hull. In *The Collected Works of C. G. Jung: Vol. 8. Structure and Dynamics of the Psyche*, 2nd ed., edited by H. Read et al., 67–91. Princeton, NJ: Princeton University Press. https://doi.org/10.1515/9781400850952.67.

Kerenyi, C. 1951. *The Gods of the Greeks*. New York: Thames & Hudson.

Linehan, M. M. 2015. *DBT Skills Training Manual*, 2nd ed. New York: Guilford Press.

Nussbaum, M. 1995. "Objectification." *Philosophy and Public Affairs* 24: 249–291. https://doi.org/10.1111/j.1088-4963.1995.tb00032.x.

Phelan, S. M., D. J. Burgess, M. W. Yeazel, W. L. Hellerstedt, J. M. Griffin, and M. van Ryn. 2015. "Impact of Weight Bias and Stigma on Quality of Care and Outcomes for Patients with Obesity." *Obesity Reviews* 16: 319–326. https://doi.org/10.1111/obr.12266.

Ponterotto, D. 2016. "Resisting the Male Gaze: Feminist Responses to the 'Normatization' of the Female Body in Western Culture." *Journal of International Women's Studies* 17: 133–151.

Rodin, J., L. Silberstein, and R. Striegel-Moore. 1984. "Women and Weight: A Normative Discontent." *Nebraska Symposium on Motivation* 32: 267–307.

Strings, S. 2019. *Fearing the Black Body: The Racial Origins of Fat Phobia*. New York: New York University Press.

Welwood, J. 2000. *Toward a Psychology of Awakening: Buddhism Psychotherapy and the Path of Personal and Spiritual Transformation*. Boston: Shambala.

Wolkstein, D., and S. N. Kramer. 1983. *Inanna: Queen of Heaven and Earth—Her Stories and Hymns from Sumer*. New York: Harper & Row.

Woodman, M. 1980. *The Owl Was a Baker's Daughter: Obesity, Anorexia Nervosa, and the Repressed Feminine*. Toronto: Inner City Books.

————. 1982. *Addiction to Perfection: The Still Unravished Bride*. Toronto: Inner City Books.

————. 1985. *The Pregnant Virgin*. Toronto: Inner City Books.

Kathryn C. Holt, PhD, LCSW, is a depth psychotherapist in private practice in Boulder, CO. She writes about bodies, motherhood, spirituality, and healing while bridging the fields of Jungian and behavioral psychology. She studied dialectical behavior therapy (DBT) at Columbia University, and is coauthor of *The Stronger Than BPD Journal*. She completed her PhD in depth psychology with a focus on Jungian and archetypal psychology, researching how people make peace with their bodies after suffering with body hatred.

Foreword writer **Anita Johnston, PhD**, is a depth psychologist, certified eating disorder specialist, and author of *Eating in the Light of the Moon*. Johnston is creator of the Light of the Moon Café, an online resource for women around the world struggling with disordered eating and body image distress. You can learn more about Johnston at www.dranitajohnston.com.

Real change *is* possible

For more than forty-five years, New Harbinger has published proven-effective self-help books and pioneering workbooks to help readers of all ages and backgrounds improve mental health and well-being, and achieve lasting personal growth. In addition, our spirituality books offer profound guidance for deepening awareness and cultivating healing, self-discovery, and fulfillment.

Founded by psychologist Matthew McKay and Patrick Fanning, New Harbinger is proud to be an independent, employee-owned company. Our books reflect our core values of integrity, innovation, commitment, sustainability, compassion, and trust. Written by leaders in the field and recommended by therapists worldwide, New Harbinger books are practical, accessible, and provide real tools for real change.

 **newharbinger**publications

MORE BOOKS from
NEW HARBINGER PUBLICATIONS

HEALING EMOTIONAL EATING FOR TRAUMA SURVIVORS

Trauma-Informed Practices to Nurture a Peaceful Relationship with Your Emotions, Body, and Food

978-1648481178 / US $19.95

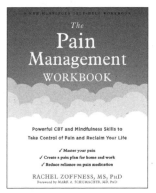

THE PAIN MANAGEMENT WORKBOOK

Powerful CBT and Mindfulness Skills to Take Control of Pain and Reclaim Your Life

978-1684036448 / US $24.95

THE EMOTIONALLY EXHAUSTED WOMAN

Why You're Feeling Depleted and How to Get What You Need

978-1648480157 / US $18.95

THE ANXIETY FIRST AID KIT

Quick Tools for Extreme, Uncertain Times

978-1684038480 / US $16.95

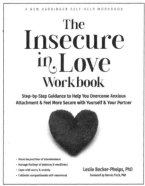

THE INSECURE IN LOVE WORKBOOK

Step-by-Step Guidance to Help You Overcome Anxious Attachment and Feel More Secure with Yourself and Your Partner

978-1648482175 / US $25.95

THE INTUITIVE EATING JOURNAL

Your Guided Journey for Nourishing a Healthy Relationship with Food

978-1684037087 / US $18.95

🌱 new**harbinger**publications

1-800-748-6273 / newharbinger.com

(VISA, MC, AMEX / prices subject to change without notice)
Follow Us 📷 📘 🐦 ▶️ 📌 in

Don't miss out on new books from New Harbinger.
Subscribe to our email list at **newharbinger.com/subscribe** 🖱️

Did you know there are **free tools** you can download for this book?

Free tools are things like **worksheets**, **guided meditation exercises**, and **more** that will help you get the most out of your book.

You can download free tools for this book—whether you bought or borrowed it, in any format, from any source—from the New Harbinger website. All you need is a NewHarbinger.com account. Just use the URL provided in this book to view the free tools that are available for it. Then, click on the "download" button for the free tool you want, and follow the prompts that appear to log in to your NewHarbinger.com account and download the material.

You can also save the free tools for this book to your **Free Tools Library** so you can access them again anytime, just by logging in to your account! Just look for this button on the book's free tools page.

+ Save this to my free tools library

If you need help accessing or downloading free tools, visit **newharbinger.com/faq** or contact us at **customerservice@newharbinger.com**.